THE COMMON MAN THROUGH THE CENTURIES

A Book of Costume Drawings

THE COMMON MAN

THROUGH

THE CENTURIES

MAX BARSIS

FREDERICK UNGAR PUBLISHING CO. *New York*

Copyright © 1973 by Frederick Ungar Publishing Co., Inc.
Printed in the United States of America
Library of Congress Catalog Card Number LC 68-31447
Designed by Irving Perkins
ISBN 0-8044-1075-5

CONTENTS

v

ABOUT THIS BOOK

FROM THE DAYS of my earliest contacts with art, the subjects that attracted me most were the ordinary, everyday people of the past—Rembrandt's beggars and ragamuffins, the peasants of Dürer and Brueghel, Hogarth's drunks and harlots, the vagabonds and gypsies of Callot. When I began to sketch, my favorite models were laborers on a scaffolding, the derelict asleep on a park bench, or groups of working men playing cards in a tavern.

Many years later, when I was working on historical costumes for one of the major Hollywood studios, I was happiest when assigned to a movie full of lower-class types. But while I never had any difficulty obtaining all of the necessary details about the costumes of kings and queens, merchant princes, or knights and their ladies, not much could be found in the books available on the kind of clothing the common people really wore. It occurred to me then that I might fulfill my ambition to publish a portfolio of sketches of the common man throughout history for a general audience, and at the same time meet the needs of researchers for stage and screen, dramatic groups, schools, colleges, and librarians.

I imagined myself roaming through the past with a sketchbook and pencil, just as other artists wander through foreign countries, drawing here a drunken peasant driven home by his wife, stopping there to sketch a barker at a fair performing for the children, or a cobbler refusing to do a hopeless repair.

Traveling in time, I could not draw from living people. I had to find my models in other centuries, in records created by their contemporaries, before I could get the facts I needed. More often than not several sources were required for one drawing. To the visual depictions of the past I added the images already in my mind after a lifetime of acquaintance with such writers as Chaucer, Villon, Cellini, Grimelshausen, Cervantes, Gustav Freytag, and many others.

In my drawings I had to keep in mind that the common man put his clothing to long, hard, continuous use. The garments often were shapeless, their original cut almost unrecognizable. For me to depict them as crisp and new would have defeated my second objective, that of illustrating the common man through the ages the way he looked—in different times and regions—as he stood and moved about, courted, transacted business, quarreled, and made merry.

A definition of the "common man" at any time in history is at best an arbitrary one. For the purposes of this book it seemed sufficient to consider as common people all those of small means, or no means, who had to struggle (although not always work!) for what at best was a modest living.

Often only traces of the magnificent upper-class costume are reflected in the more slowly changing dress of the ordinary people. Therefore, for a picture of the dominant costume of various historic periods the reader should occasionally refer to one of the general costume books that deal essentially with upper-class costume.

My sketchbook begins with later Roman days (preceded by a few Greek examples necessary for an understanding of the Roman period) and ends with the French Revolution. The geographical scope is limited to Europe, from England to the eastern border of the old German Empire. It is this area which, for simplicity's sake, in the following pages is called "Europe." American costume has not been included. Most of American dress was the common man's costume, and has been treated extensively and competently in several special books, to which I could have added nothing.

For me, this has been a pleasant journey over many years, but it could hardly have been accomplished without the help and guidance of many people. Thanks are due especially to Professor Karl Maria Swoboda of the University of Vienna for his never-failing advice on questions relating to the history of art; to Mrs. Lucie Hampel, head of the fashion collections of the City of Vienna, for her assistance on all technical points of dressmaking; to Dr. Annamaria Farnarano of the Centro Internazionale delle Arti e del Costume, Venice; to Professor Enrique Perez, Comendador, of the Academia San Fernando, Madrid; to Mrs. E.E. Harkavy (Millia Davenport) for much invaluable advice and criticism; and to all the many libraries without whose generous help I would never have found my way.

M.B.

ON THE SOURCES
FOR THIS BOOK

WHILE THE MEN and women who people my drawings are, in some ways, the products of my imagination, every detail of their costume is the result of careful research. Since sources of costume information for the common man are often scarce, fragmentary, and obscure, my drawings for a single costume are frequently based on more than one source.

When I first began seriously to search out these sources, I found that the most difficult part of the problem was to understand what kind of source material was available, since it quickly became apparent that this material often would be different from what could be found, much more easily, for upper-class dress. I also discovered that the problem had to be solved differently for different periods; a type of source material good for the fifteenth century might be useless, or nonexistent, for the ninth century. Once this general question was settled, locating individual sources of a specific kind was comparatively easy.

Since others interested in the subject may be faced with the same problem, I think it may be helpful to describe here the groups of sources I found useful for the various periods, and to quote some of the individual examples for each group. This is by no means a complete list of existing sources or even of those used here; basically it is a guide to researchers indicating where some of the more practicable trails begin.

The figures in the drawings are based only occasionally on one specific source. In most cases they represent a general image of people of the respective rank, profession, and nationality as it emerges out of the comparison of various sources of this period. For this reason, in the following description of such sources, reference to a specific drawing is made only when a specific source is named in the text.

Costume sources for Greek and Roman antiquity present no problem, particularly since the costume of the common man consisted in that time of only a few rarely changing components. Information on Greek costume and the everyday life of the people can be found on vases and other pottery in the Greek collections in most of the larger museums of Europe and the United States. Among the most extensive are the collections of the Metropolitan Museum of Art in New York, the Museo Nazionale in Naples, and the British Museum in London.

Greek and Roman statuary is another source for costumes of antiquity. Some of the statues are to be found in their original locations, others in museums, including, in addition to those mentioned above, the Museo Laterano in Rome and the Museo Archaeologico in Sicily.

The best costume sources for ancient Rome are the murals of Pompeii and Herculaneum. Although these are first-century (A.D.) examples, the stability of the Roman costume, particularly that of the common people, means that this source can be considered valid in general for several centuries before and after their date of execution.

With the approaching Dark Ages, sources become scarcer and scarcer, and finally disappear altogether. The examples of the costume of Germanic tribes to be seen on the victory columns of the Roman emperors, notably those of Trajan and Marcus Aurelius, although dating back to the second century, probably give us a fairly good idea of the common man's costume for several centuries to come. The reader is referred to the later Roman costume on page 12.

In the ninth century, with the beginning of the new Carolingian civilization, sources begin to reappear. The occasional primitive drawings and paintings that have survived are of little value for our purpose, but one can find an occasional ivory book cover, a plaque, or even pieces of early church sculpture with useable information. In the tenth and eleventh centuries the art of the illuminated manuscript came into its own, and illustrated missals, psalters, and calendaria such as those of the Echternach or Reichenau schools or the Gerona Codex are among the best of the otherwise rare sources for the common man's costume.

These sources are more frequent in the centuries that follow; some examples are Queen Mary's Psalter (twelfth century), the Luttrel Psalter and the Wellyslav bible (fourteenth century), the Breviary of Martin of Aragon (circa 1400), the sacramentaries of Limoges, and calendars like those in the Ambraser collection in Vienna.

Early ecclesiastical paintings contain few figures of ordinary people, but they offer some helpful information, in murals such as those in the church Saint Savin sur Gartemps, Vienne, the altarpiece of the "Meister der Goldenen Tafel," both twelfth century, or even in painted figures to be found in some of the very early small Romanesque churches, such as those of Puergg and Ramsau in Upper Austria. A more fertile source, however, may be found in sculpture as, for example, in the Cathedral of Autun (twelfth century) and the very instructive figures in the Church of San Marco, Venice, representing the labors of the twelve months (thirteenth and fourteenth centuries). In using these sources we should remember that tribal and regional traces had all but vanished by the year 1000 and that one general style of costume prevailed all over Europe. We may therefore assume that a source for one country is valid for all.

Costumes in representations of biblical subjects may safely be taken to be those worn in the artist's own time. This holds true roughly up to the middle of the sixteenth century. See page 187. Examples of paintings of the fourteenth and fifteenth centuries offering useable detail are those by Andrea de Firenze, Vittore Carpaccio, Jan van Eyck, Hans Memling, Sandro Botticelli, Jehan Fouquet, M. Reichlich, Mathias Grünewald, and—the most important for our subject—Giotto di Bondone. See page 31. Figures in stained glass windows, for example those in the Cathedral of Moulins or the Church of Nôtre Dame de Semur or the Cathedral of Chartres, are also sources for this period. But generally, again, drawings, woodcuts and engravings offer more information than paintings.

In the thirteenth century secular literature makes its appearance, with illustrations that here and there offer a good, if somewhat thin source for our subject. Among the useful works are the *Romans d'aventure* of the thirteenth and following centuries, as for example, the *Roman de la rose* by Guillaume de Lorris, *Le Roman fauvel* (fourteenth century), and the *Histoire de Lancelot* (fifteenth century). The various illustrations published in the fifteenth century for the works of Giovanni Boccaccio, one of the most popular authors of the preceding century, are a rich source of information about the common man's dress and appearance.

Beginning with the thirteenth century, we find even more useful material in illustrated chronicles of contemporary events: *Weltchronik* by Rudolf von Ems (thirteenth century), Jehan Froissart's *Chronique de France et d'Angleterre* (fourteenth), and John Lydgate's *The Pilgrimage of Man* (early fifteenth), Jean de Wavrin's *Chronique d'Angleterre* (late fifteenth), and *The Travels of Sir John Mandeville* (early fifteenth).

Tapestries are an additional source of enlightenment, for example those of the city of Reims (late fifteenth century) and the tapestries illustrating the *Histoire de St. Etienne* in the Musée Cluny in Paris.

The first mentioned offer considerable information on the appearance of beggars and vagrants. Another good source on the poorest classes is the *Liber Vagatorum*, a late fifteenth-century book about beggars and vagrants. See page 88.

The richest source for the sixteenth century are the Books of Hours of princes and other great figures, so called because they were collections of prayers in the sequence of the hours of devotion, illustrated with beautiful miniatures by excellent artists. Besides showing ordinary people as background participants in religious events, whole pages are sometimes devoted to the life and labors of the common people. They also appear often in decorative bywork. Among the most remarkable of these books are the *Hours* of Marguerite d'Orleans, the *Très Riches Heures* of Jean, Duc de Berry, the *Hours* of Charles d'Angoulême, the *Hours* of Queen Isabella of Spain, and the *Breviary* of Cardinal Grimani of Venice. These illustrations show a certain uniformity of costume since they are all the work of Flemish artists or of artists trained in the Flemish manner, and also because at that time Flemish-Burgundian fashions were prevalent all over Europe. See pages 118 and 119.

The change to German styles, which would dominate much of Europe for a good part of the sixteenth century, took place only slowly, and in some countries the lot of the common man was affected only minimally. The best source for these German fashions are the woodcuts, engravings, and some of the paintings of Germany's greatest master, Albrecht Dürer, and those of his followers. See pages 129 and 130. Other great illustrators of people's life in this period are Hans Holbein the Younger and the Swiss Urs Graf, with his magnificent representations of the lansquenets, the mercenary soldiers who had an important influence on the century's costume.

Another very rich source for the beginning of the sixteenth century are the illustrations of city chronicles, like those of Swiss cities by Diebold Schilling or, a little earlier, of the Council of Konstanz by Ulrich Richental. The Behaim Codex in Cracow also belongs in this group. See page 112.

The big German peasant uprising of 1524–1525 and the unrest of the preceding years saw the appearance of leaflets pro and con with valuable pictorial material.

Spanish costume information may be found in illustrations to *Peligros del Mondo* (Saragoza, 1531) by Juan de Capua.

In the Netherlands during the first half of the sixteenth century, the engraver Lucas van Leyden found much inspiration in the looks of peasants and other common folk. See page 119. He was followed by an artist whose name comes to mind first when researching sources for the common people's dress—Pieter Brueghel the Elder. See page 152. A contemporary of Brueghel was Pieter Aertsen, to whom we owe excellent details on town, especially market, people. A similar role was played at the same time in Italy by Bartolomeo Passarotti and, for peasant life, by Jacopo Bassano.

In the first half of the sixteenth century a book appeared that is unique for our purpose, showing the first traces of regional costume: the *Trachtenbuch* (Book of Local Costumes) by Christoph Weiditz based on his voyages to Spain (1525) and the Netherlands (1531–1532). The original is in the Germanisches Museum in Nuremberg. See page 107.

A very informative book devoted to the appearance of the lower classes was published in the second half of the century: Jost Amman's *Staendebuch* (1568), which called itself "a description of all classes on earth," but really deals only with German people, with rhymes by Hans Sachs. See page 114.

The most important and comprehensive book of this kind is Cesare Vecellio's *Degli Habiti antichi et moderni di diversi parti del Mondo, etc.* (Old and Modern Costumes of Various Parts of the World), issued in 1590, which deals in illustrations and text with people of many ranks and professions in many places of Europe and elsewhere. The representations of costumes in Central and West Europe seem for the most part to be authentic, but some of the others appear to be products of pure imagination.

Of a similar nature are the sixteenth-century books by Ferdinando Bertelli, Jean Jacques Boissard, and Abraham de Bruyn, and, reaching into the next century, Georgius Braun's *Contrafactur and Beschreibung der vornembsten Staedt der Welt* (Depiction and Description of the World's Most Important Towns), published from 1574 to 1618. A specialized work giving excellent information on the dress and life of the miners in the Tyrol, but valid also for those of other parts, is the *Schwazer Bergbuch* of 1556 (Innsbruck, Ferdinandeum). Here we also find Emperor Maximilian I's *Weisskunig* and his *Jagd- und Fischereibuch* (Book of Hunting and Fishing), both containing good illustrations of common people at many occupations and crafts. For the costumes of artisans, we have the official *Bürger und Meisterbuch* of Nuremberg (1534–1651).

An invaluable French source for lower-class urban types, but occasionally also the rural, are the volumes of the *Cris de Paris* (Cries Heard in the Streets of Paris), published for the first time in the sixteenth century. In the seventeenth century their most important contributors were members of the engraving family Bonnart. See page 246. The *Cris de Paris* are collected in the Musée Carnavalet in Paris.

By the seventeenth century, more artists were interested in depicting contemporary life on its lower levels. Most important is the work of the French artist Jacques Callot showing the lowest classes (see page 204). Also in France, and at almost the same time, we find two of the few easel painters of the Baroque who chose for their subject the peasant and his surroundings, Louis Le Nain and his brother Antoine (see page 230). Among other French sources are the illustrations of an early seventeenth-century book, *Proverbes joyeux de Lagnet*, and illustrated ballads published by F. Gerard in the Bibliotheque Nationale, Paris.

Illustrated ballads are also a good source for the English common man's costume in the first half of the seventeenth century, especially those in the collection of the Roxburghe Club. See pages 202 and 280. Extensive information on English middle-class costume of the same period is to be found in the work of the Bohemian-born engraver Wenceslaus Hollar. The engravings of Mathias Merian are one of the sources for German costume.

For Italy we have the graphic work of Annibale Carracci at the end of the sixteenth century (see page 187), and in the seventeenth century his imitator Giuseppe Mittelli and Michelangelo Cerquozzi. The Dutch painter Pieter van Lier, who lived in Rome, has given us a delightful portrait of Roman life in taverns and other public places. Antonio Vassilacchi portrayed Venetian life in the late sixteenth and early seventeenth centuries.

Spanish popular costume of the seventeenth as well as the following century may be found in the aforementioned books dealing with Europe as well as in engraved costume sheets in the Academia San Fernando, and in the national and the municipal libraries in Madrid. Another source is one of Spain's greatest painters, Diego Velazquez. See page 229.

In no other century is there such an abundance of information on peasant costume as there is in the work of the seventeenth-century peasant painters of the Netherlands: Adriaen van Ostade, David Teniers, Cornelis Bega, Cornelis Dusart, Philips Wouwerman, Nicholaes Berchem, and others. See page 252.

By the beginning of the eighteenth century, all over Europe, local difference in the costume of the common people, which to a certain degree had developed during the preceding century, had vanished in towns (with some exceptions in Italy and Spain). In the rural areas such differences did not disappear before the middle of the eighteenth century, and even then never completely. At the same time, the number of pictorial representations of urban life increased to the point where it really is no longer a problem to locate any detail in the costume, by now more or less uniform, of lower-class town people. French artists who did engravings of the life on the lower levels include Jean Baptiste Pater, Edmé Bouchardon, François Boucher, Hubert F. Gravelot, Jean Baptiste Greuze, and Jean Michel Moreau le Jeune. Domestic servants are charmingly portrayed in the paintings of Jean Baptiste Chardin. A rich collection of all material on the French Revolution is to be found in the Musée Carnavalet in Paris.

Although artistically the German illustrators of the period generally do not live up to the French, Daniel Chodowiecki's engravings are an inexhaustible source for middle-class costume. See page 335. Other sources include Johann Esaias Nilson, Joseph Franz von Goez, Johann Seekatz, and Johann Eleazar Schenau.

Of all the artists of any age who observed and represented aspects of the common people and their costume, none surpassed England's William Hogarth. See page 277. Another good English source for the second half of the eighteenth century is George Morland.

Among the territories that make up present-day Italy, the most fertile for our purpose is Venice, particularly because of the remarkable colored drawings of Giovanni Grevenbroeck II. See page 294. An illustrated book by Domenico Louisa, *Il Teatro Veneziano*, 1710, and another, *Le Arti che vanno per la via nella citta di Venezia* (The Arts in the Streets of Venice), 1788, are both in the city museum of Venice. The paintings of Pietro Longhi are also a cornucopia of Venice's lower-class people's dress.

Tuscan material can be found in the *Proverbi Toscani* by Giuseppe Pittoli in the library of the Museo degli Arti e Tradizioni Populari in Rome, which offers much information on Italian peasant costume. For the kindgom of Naples there are Pietro Fabris' *Raccolta di varii vestimenti ed arti del regno di Napoli* (Presentation of Various Vestments and Arts of the Kingdom of Naples), 1773, and a book by Theodore Viero, *Raccolta di 126 Stampe* (Presentation of 126 Prints) 1783–1791, which also has material on Spain and other European nations. There are also in Italy, of course, many typical eighteenth-century engravers in whose work material useable for our subject may occasionally be found, such as, for example, Francesco Magiotto.

The most distinguished and one of the richest

sources of Spanish people's costume in the eighteenth century is the work of the century's greatest Spanish painter, Francisco Goya.

In the eighteenth century, also, many European cities had collections of prints done in imitation of the *Cris de Paris*; these are an incomparable source for our subject. See page 342.

Finally I come to the problem child of this book, a problem because the subject is much too extensive for it—the regional dress of the sixteenth, seventeenth, and eighteenth centuries. Regional costume started some time at the beginning of the sixteenth century, and was strongest in Germany, Austria, Spain, and the Scandinavian countries. Never very remarkable in town, these regional styles had disappeared in such areas almost completely by the beginning of the eighteenth century, whereas in rural areas, they underwent a strong development during the first decades of the century, only to follow the urban example in the second half. But a most emphatic comeback and new development occurred toward the end of the eighteenth century and continued through the first half of the nineteenth. It is this kind of costume that generally is known as European peasant costume; in some places it can be seen even today, although mostly for the benefit of tourists. See pages 318 and 335.

This last and most extensive development falls outside the scope of this book, which ends with the French Revolution. But even earlier periods produced such an enormous variety of costumes, differing not only from country to country, but from valley to valley and village to village, that their treatment would fill a work of many volumes and take the lifetime of many regional costume specialists. On the other hand, these costumes without doubt were a part, and an important part, of the common man's appearance. Within the limitations of my sketchbook, I have tried to offer, by a few samples, at least a glimpse of this kind of costume and to name a few sources covering these examples.

The most easily accessible material seems to be in the German area. A copious and thorough compilation is to be found in Friedrich Hottenroth's *Deutsche Volkstrachten, Staedtisch und Laendlich, vom XVI Jahrhundert bis zum Anfang des XIX Jahrhunderts* (German Regional Costume, Urban and Rural, from the XVI Century to the Beginning of the XIX Century), Frankfurt am Main, 1898–1901. This source also quotes many special sources for single territories, as, for instance, *Nürnbergische Kleidertrachten der Manns und Weibpersonen*, 1689, Heinrich Glaser's *Basler Kleidung*, and others.

Other fertile sources are Johann Martin Will's *Sammlung Europäischer Kleider Trachten*, 1780, and Abraham of Santa Clara's *Neu Eröffnete Welt Gallerie*, 1708. Such source books for German and other European regional costume can often be found not only in the big national or city libraries, but also in small libraries attached to folklore museums, sometimes even in very obscure places. In such museums one may also occasionally discover original pieces of common people's wardrobe, generally only those of durable material, such as buckles, buttons, belts, even shoes.

For France a work by Jacques Grasset de Saint Sauveur, *Encyclopédie des voyages* (1795–96), illustrates the major part of French peasant costume of the later eighteenth century. Examples of earlier books of the century are Seiboth's *Costumes des femmes de Strassbourgh* et *Alsace Française*.

The sources quoted above as general sources for Italian and Spanish regional costume also contain representations of local peasant costume. A rare collection that I found in the British Museum is *Italian Peasant Costume* by Giovanni Azzerboni (1790).

Books on Scandinavian local costume of the seventeenth and eighteenth century may be seen in the Lipperheide costume library (Freiherr v. Lipperheidesche Kostüm Bibliothek, now part of the Staatsbibliothek, West Berlin): one by Jacob Rieter for Denmark, one by Sved Herrestad and K.V. Svedman on Sweden, one by J. Senn on Norway, and one on Iceland by E. Olafsen.

Besides the libraries mentioned above, others specializing in costume or with a department of costumes are the Metropolitan Museum of Art in New York and the library of the Centro Internationale delle Arti e Costume in Venice, which offer invaluable sources for further research on the clothing of the common man to any reader who may want to go more deeply into this field.

Ancient Greece and Rome

HUNTER AND ARTISAN
GREECE. FOURTH CENTURY B.C.

Our series of drawings of the common man begins with a blacksmith, right, whose costume is the one shown in illustrations of the Greek and Roman god Hephaistos (called Vulcan by the Romans), who forged a net strong enough to catch his wife and the god of war as they lay together. Hephaistos, the god of fire and protector of artisans, used his forge to make tools and household items as well as weapons for the immortals on Olympus.

Two of the most characteristic articles of clothing worn by working men in ancient times appear in this drawing. The blacksmith's cap, or pileus, is made of felt or leather and could be round or conical in shape. One corner of his tunic (chiton) has been untied to allow him greater freedom of movement and later would come already made that way for working people, with one shoulder bare (exomis).

The hunter, who offers his spear for inspection, is wearing a type of short-sleeved chiton common to all classes. His cloak (chlamys) is also a classless garment and will continue to be worn for many centuries. Both men are wearing laced shoes turned down at the top.

TRAVELER AND CRAFTSMAN
GREECE. FOURTH CENTURY B.C.

Our traveler, left, resembles his patron Hermes (Mercury to the Romans), who was not only swift of foot but an expert at sleight of hand. He earned his reputation for speed and cunning before he was a day old by flying down from Olympus on his winged sandals, stealing fifty head of Apollo's cattle, hiding them in a cave, and returning undetected to his cradle. The traveler's wide-brimmed hat was characteristic of the Greeks, whose occupations exposed them to sun and rain. His rather long chiton is kept tucked up in two places, his chest and around his waist, by a strap, a Greek pattern often seen on pottery, but not usually adopted by the Romans. His cape is attached by straps to his shoulders; his sandals are attached to his feet by thongs.

The craftsman, right, working in a shop, probably belonged to the poorer class because wealthy shopowners employed slaves to do their work for them often in large stores. His sole garment consists of two pieces of cloth wrapped around the hips. The top one is weighted at the lower corners with a metal ornament to preserve the draping.

DOMESTIC SERVANTS

GREECE. FIFTH TO THIRD CENTURY B.C.

The Greeks had many slaves, most of whom belonged to tribes less civilized than their masters. They were generally well treated, and there were no slave uprisings such as took place later in Rome.

We assume the women in these drawings to be slaves because free women rarely carried water or, for that matter, did any domestic work other than spinning, weaving, and sewing. The ankle-length chiton in the patterned fabric is of a simple cut and just wide enough at the hem to allow movement of the feet. This girl has draped a long, soft scarf around her shoulders and arms. Her companion on the right is wearing two chitons, a short one over a long one. Both are tied around her body at the waist. The materials used for such garments were either linen or wool.

BAKERY SHOP WORKERS
ROME. FIRST CENTURY A.D.

Every visitor to Pompeii is attracted by the sight of the well-preserved ovens to be found at various points of the excavations. Every provincial Roman town had its bakery shops, and during the reign of Augustus there were in Rome itself more than three hundred of them. The bakers produced a fine white bread for the wealthy, but for the poor black bread of a rather inferior quality and a coarse white bread that was not much better.

Both men and women of the lower classes wore, frequently as their only garment, tunics of linen or wool, usually undyed. Working men often wore their tunics unbelted, even outside the house, a practice considered uncouth by the upper classes.

COPPERSMITH AND COOK

ROME. FIRST CENTURY A.D.

Craftsmen, like this coppersmith, left, and vendors of all kinds of products sold their merchandise from workshops or stalls set up in the forum or the markets. The foodseller here seems to be trying to entice a buyer to purchase his wares.

Though it was the privilege of every free-born Roman, whatever his estate, to wear the toga, which we consider the characteristic garment of the Romans, none of the citizens in any of these drawings is wearing one. The explanation is simple: the average poor person could not afford the expense of a garment made of several yards of fine wool. Therefore, both at home and in the streets, common people generally wore only tunics. The practice was so prevalent that the poor were known as "populus tunicatus."

SLAVE GIRL AND WOMAN
OF THE PEOPLE
ROME. FIRST CENTURY A.D.

The only domestic work done by a wealthy Roman woman was weaving and spinning, and even a poor free woman, right, performed only light chores. Everything else was done by slave girls like the water carrier seen here, left, who was probably put to work while still a child. A slave was sometimes freed when she was old, but even then she might keep on working as a housekeeper.

Over their tunics, free women wore a big, rectangular cloak, the palla, often elaborately draped and made of costly cloth. The palla evolved from the earlier stola, a similar, though wider and heavier, garment.

In the case of a lower-class woman, like the one shown here, the palla was represented by a shoulder shawl, of coarse material, for protection in bad weather. In general, the only other garment she wore was her tunic, and she probably slept in that too.

STREET PLAYERS

ROME. FIRST CENTURY A.D.

These actors are performing a comedy for the crowd in a Roman square. They are probably using a quickly improvised stage, much like those on which Etruscan actors performed as early as the fourth century B.C. Their masks and hairstyles are, however, typical of the Greek stage.

The arts of music, drawing, and acting were brought to Rome from Etruria, Greece, and the Greek colonies in Asia Minor and Sicily. The great period of the Roman stage was the last quarter of the first century B.C., but even then it was the gladiators' arena, not the theater, that attracted the masses.

SHOP WORKERS

ROME. FIRST CENTURY A.D.

Much of Roman industry was based on the specialized, and often highly skilled work of slaves who were generally prisoners of war or inhabitants of conquered territories.

These slaves seen here are working in a textile plant. As proved by the murals at Pompeii, the slaves'

costumes were no different from those of the lower-class free Romans—tunics of various types, sometimes worn one on top of the other. But, unlike the Greeks, free Romans, even of very low rank, never went barefoot.

TOWNSMEN
ROME. FIRST CENTURY A.D.

In bad weather, a Roman townsman might wear a cucullus, a hood with a short cape attached, left. Of military origin, and reportedly brought to Rome by legionaries returning from Germany, the cucullus remained for centuries a part of the wardrobe of the common man throughout Europe.

The wrapper known as the paenula, worn by the other man, also originated with the army. At this date it was worn by mule drivers, sedan bearers, peasants, and other people whose work kept them out of doors. Later it replaced the toga, even among people of rank. Both the cucullus and the paenula were originally made of strong, heavy material, such as hairy wool or leather.

11

MULE DRIVER AND PEASANT
ROME, EARLY CHRISTIAN ERA

The small farmer, right, who cultivated the fields was also the backbone of the conquering Roman army. When the wars of conquest became almost uninterrupted, the peasant-soldier on his long absences from home discovered there were easier ways of making a living than the hard work of the fields. As he abandoned it his place was taken by a continuous stream of slaves from the conquered countries. Agricultural production also changed. The result was the formation of the latifundia—estates which grew to sometimes enormous size under the early emperors, and were farmed by slaves. Only in the north did some small farming survive.

In the past, rural slaves had shared the simple life of their masters. Now, on the latifundia, slaves like the mule driver, left, were treated at best like prisoners, and at worst like animals. Note the contrast between the way the slave and the peasant are dressed.

CLERK AND WOMAN SHOPPER
ROME. FIRST CENTURY A.D.

As all sources show, Roman men of all classes wore their hair short. We usually imagine them as smooth-shaven, but this was not the case in the early days or under certain emperors who set the fashion for beards. Actually, many poor men let their beards grow to save the trouble and expense of shaving.

Shopowners and other businessmen of some means spent most of their day in the forum and other public places, leaving the work to employees, who might be either free men or slaves.

The woman shopper in this drawing, right, wears only a tunic and around her head a kerchief. Free women did their own shopping for everything but food. This was done by their servants, who were generally slaves.

CONSTRUCTION WORKERS
ROME. EARLY CHRISTIAN ERA

Romans used to consider trousers the mark of barbarians. However, during the long cold winters in Germany and Gaul, the legionaries discovered that trousers came in very handy. Although they first brought them back to Rome in the third century, it was not until the fifth that the long Germanic leggings shown here came into general use. The Romans had earlier adopted the short Gallic breeches, or braccae.

Considering the climate of Italy in winter, which, contrary to its reputation, is by no means clement, the trousers must have been a welcome addition to Roman dress.

GERMANIC TRIBESMEN
SECOND CENTURY A.D.

The men in this drawing are barbarians, which was what Greeks and Romans called people of civilizations other than their own.

In general, the Germanic tribesmen who were in contact with Rome had begun to dress like lower-class Romans. Their long hair, however, was entirely un-Roman, and their shoes, made of pieces of leather turned up at the edges and fastened with a net of narrow straps, differed from the Roman sandals. In the days of the Emperors Trajan and Marcus Aurelius, whose victory columns are the source for these costumes, Romans had not yet adopted the Germanic trousers.

In battle, Germanic tribesmen took off their jackets and tied them around their waists. Since they were often depicted that way, it has sometimes been erroneously assumed that they normally went about with naked upper bodies.

GERMANIC TRIBESWOMEN
SECOND CENTURY A.D.

The Roman influence on the Germanic tribes extended to the dress of women as well as men.

The woman of the house made all of the clothing —jackets, trousers, stockings, and coats for the men; for herself, long tunics and, sometimes, cloaks similar to those worn by the men in the previous drawing. The materials used were linen, leather, or wool (loden cloth). Fur was also used in winter.

Ninth to Fourteenth Centuries

PHYSICIAN AND WARRIOR
CAROLINGIAN EMPIRE. MID-NINTH CENTURY

By the time of this drawing, Charlemagne had built up his formidable empire, and raised his subjects to a comparatively high level of civilization. Medicine, formerly the province of the monks, was now a profession for laymen, too, and was much practiced by Arabs and Jews. Women shared in the work of collecting salutary herbs and preparing ointments and tinctures.

Costumes of both the upper and lower classes had lost whatever regional distinctions may have existed during the migration of peoples and were pretty much the same throughout Europe. Trousers were generally worn by men of the lower classes, but the leg bands on this soldier, left, once typical for many Germanic tribes, were now rarely seen.

PEASANTS

CAROLINGIAN EMPIRE. MID-NINTH CENTURY

Soon after the *Völkerwanderung,* or migration of peoples, ending in the downfall of the Roman Empire, many a small landowner lost all his possessions to a noble and became his serf. He dressed in nothing but a coarse smock, often with no covering for his head and no shoes. His wife, who wore a similar smock, might wrap some clothes around her head and shoulders.

The source for this drawing was an ivory book cover of the ninth century, probably Frankish, in the Bargello in Florence. Ivory work of this kind was a medium favored by monastic artists of that day. One of the most famous of those who carved in ivory was Tuotilo of St. Gallen, who was also an architect, goldsmith, and craftsman in other precious metals. The Virgin Mary, according to legend, had been seen assisting him in his work and handing him his tools.

GERMAN MEN
TENTH CENTURY

In the tenth century, free, small farmers still survived in many parts of Germany, including Saxony, Frisia, and some valleys of the Alps, but their number was in steady decline. In the newly revived towns, however, a new generation of free workers came into existence. The men in this drawing belong without doubt to a low stratum of early Middle Age society, but it would be hard to tell from their appearance whether they are free peasants, serfs or rural slave laborers, or townsmen, since such differences had not yet found expression in dress.

PEASANT AND BOY

SPAIN. TENTH CENTURY

In those parts of Europe which were Roman or Romanized before the arrival of the Germanic invaders, Roman peasant dress styles survived for many centuries. On the man in this drawing we see the old felt hat, or pileus, and the virtually unchanged cloak and tunic. The boy is wearing a tunic. The sole local variation seems to be in the slits in the skirt of the man's tunic.

LABORERS
FRANCE. CIRCA 1100

In the early twelfth century the building trade was experiencing a tremendous boom. Just as in our time the air is filled with the noise of bulldozers and concrete mixers, in those days the sound of hammers, axes, and saws reverberated through the towns. Earlier, the building crafts had been limited pretty much to erecting and enlarging castles and churches. Now they were called upon to work on the new and quickly expanding towns. Old Roman cities, never quite dead, revived and new ones grew around the strongholds of the nobles.

In this drawing, the laborer on the left is wearing a fitted smock and trousers, consisting of two separate leg-pieces fastened to a strap around the waist. The man on the right is wearing a smock with a broad band of trim at the neckline.

PEASANTS
FRANCE. TWELFTH CENTURY

In twelfth-century literature the peasant was not yet idealized, as he would be—very much in contrast to reality—by French poets in later centuries. On the contrary, a typical contemporary description described the peasant as "an ugly monster, an animal black as charcoal with a shaggy head, a flat nose, turned-up nostrils revealing big yellow teeth, dressed in dirty, torn, patched-up clothes which leave him half naked." Right up to the eighteenth century, peasants are described as wild, cunning, unbridled, rude, clumsy, obstinate, malicious, and so forth. We must, however, remember that they themselves could not write, and all we know about them was written by their arch-enemies, the nobles and the townspeople.

In this drawing, the wife is bringing food to her husband at work in the fields. French peasants ate their meals at nine in the morning and three in the afternoon. Their diet consisted of a mush of beans, lentils, millet, or oats, and a bitter bread made of rye, barley, or oats and full of bran and weeds. It is possible they also had eggs, and at slaughtering time in the late autumn, they sometimes had pork. Their drink was water or beer made from rye or barley.

PEASANTS

ENGLAND. TWELFTH CENTURY

By the twelfth century the number of free peasants in England had declined considerably from Anglo-Saxon days and the new class of free yeomen had not yet arisen. The two men in our drawing are serfs. Although they had no right to leave the land to which they were bound, they did have certain rights under the law, such as that of cutting timber to build their cabins and collecting wood and breaking off branches for firewood.

In these costumes, which I took from Queen Mary's Psalter and other manuscripts in the British Museum, we once again meet the old Roman hood, or cucullus, right. Now and for a long time to come, under the name of capuchon in England, chaperon in France, or Gugel in Germany, it will be one of the most commonly seen styles of headgear for men and, to a lesser degree, women. The hood of the man to the left is dangling down his back, ready to be pulled up under his hat if need be.

SHEPHERDS

GERMANY AND ENGLAND. TWELFTH CENTURY

We owe much of our knowledge of early medieval peasant costume to the fact that shepherds were present at the Nativity and that medieval artists portrayed their subjects in contemporary garb. In the Psalter in which I found these tunics and hoods, they were depicted in light blues and reds. The painters were probably more concerned with decorative effect than veracity because, as we know from later sources, the linen or hemp, mostly used, was rarely dyed. Wool too was usually left in its natural undyed gray, brown, or white state.

26

JEWS
GERMANY. THIRTEENTH CENTURY

These two men face a hostile world. Before the twelfth century Jews took part in Christian economic life and were not confined to a ghetto. Mob violence was rare. Charlemagne used Jewish diplomats and Louis the Pious had a Jewish court physician. The murderous persecutions of the twelfth century began at Wurzburg in 1147 and in England in 1190.

It was the Lateran Council of 1215 which first decreed a distinct mode of dress for Jews—the white and/or orange hats shown here. The other indication that these men are Jews is their long hair and beards. Also, although they are obviously poor, they are wearing their tunics longer than customary among other poor people. In these illustrations, taken from a Latin Psalter in the National Library in Vienna, the clothes are depicted in light greens or blues and yellows.

PEASANTS
ENGLAND. THIRTEENTH CENTURY

The life of the bonded peasant was a hard one indeed, as these drawings adapted from contemporary manuscripts in the British Museum clearly show. In addition to tilling his own land, the bonded peasant had to till his lord's, and perform many other duties for him as well. He also had to get his lord's permission for almost every important decision he took, including marriage, and often had to pay a fee for obtaining this consent. On his death the serf's best head of cattle fell to the lord. But his draft animals were worked so hard and fed so poorly that they were very small, about half the size of today's cattle.

PEASANTS
ITALY. THIRTEENTH CENTURY

Looking at these two men, we should keep in mind that these were the days when knighthood was in flower. Along with courtly manners, luxurious courtly dress had developed for the nobles. Not a trace of that can be found in the garb of the common man. Among Italian peasants the old Roman dress remained virtually unchanged.

WOMAN AND GRAIN DEALER
ITALY. THIRTEENTH AND FOURTEENTH CENTURIES

The grain being purchased here is probably wheat, millet, or corn. In northern countries, it would be oats or lentils. Rice was not unknown either.

Food, like other merchandise, was sold in markets or from stalls set up in streets. Sometimes there were so many stalls that the passageway on the streets became almost too narrow for people on horseback to get by. Prices, measures, and even the quality of the products came under government regulation.

SHEPHERDS
ITALY. FOURTEENTH CENTURY

In rural communities shepherds were always held in high regard. They were not only responsible for the community's most valuable possessions, but also knew about all kinds of remedies for human ailments.

The paintings of Giotto di Bondone, who lived from approximately 1256–1337, were my sources for the clothes in this drawing. The son of a poor Italian peasant, Giotto very much enjoyed the company of shepherds, peasants, and similar folk, just as Brueghel was to do in the sixteenth century. Giotto was one of the first painters to portray such people realistically, in their actual costumes, with the smallest details observed.

31

DESTITUTE COUPLE
ITALY. FOURTEENTH CENTURY

In the Middle Ages throughout Europe it was considered a moral duty to cloth the "bashful poor," and many fraternal societies ordered their members to distribute garments to the poor on certain days of the year. Other groups took care of old people. Some tailors' guilds in France, for instance, had a rule that journeymen guilty of negligence had to work one day without pay, and repair the clothes of the poor. The goldsmiths in some French cities kept one of their shops open every Sunday and on Apostles' Day; the profits were used to arrange an Easter dinner for the poor.

DOMESTIC SERVANTS
FRANCE. FOURTEENTH CENTURY

An elderly nurse, right, and her young helper try to keep the scion of the noble house in a good mood. The wages for women performing domestic chores were regulated by governmental decree. There even existed special employment agencies to mediate their services. Before hiring a servant, one was warned to make careful inquiries as to whether she drank, stole, or had been fired for a serious offense. Young servant girls were not allowed to be lodged in rooms with low windows or in attics with roof windows, presumably because it was too easy to climb in and out of them.

Both of these women, whom I found depicted on French miniatures in the Bibliothèque Nationale in Paris, are wearing short-sleeved surcots over their long tunics. Although a young girl might leave her hair uncovered when she was working in the house, women generally wore veils over their heads inside the house as well as outdoors.

MASKED REVELERS

FRANCE. FOURTEENTH CENTURY

At certain times, a "fair of the fools" was celebrated in the cities. It started in a church, but soon spilled out into the streets and often got out of hand. The revelers, in many disguises, some of them quite vulgar, pestered passersby with their often cruel pranks.

MASKED REVELERS
FRANCE. FOURTEENTH CENTURY

On some occasions, stages were built in public
squares and shows were performed by townsmen of
all classes. The whole town would turn out for these
affairs, and the masked figures could create mischief
with little fear of punishment.

MINSTRELS

FRANCE. FOURTEENTH CENTURY

Imagine a castle deep in the snow. For weeks, even months, hardly a solitary pilgrim has passed by. One is cut off completely from the world and its diversions. Suddenly there is the sound of approaching voices, tunes played on a lute, a flute, or a psalterium—the minstrels are coming!

In the Middle Ages, they were entertainers, singers, poets, newspapers, and magazines, all in one.

The bagpiper is wearing a smock cut in the new Burgundian style, closely fitted with a very loose belt. This was a fairly typical outfit for a lower-class townsman in the middle of the fourteenth century. The other man is wearing a monklike cowl. Many runaway monks, as well as down-at-the-heel clerics, did indeed join the minstrels.

JUGGLERS
FRANCE. FOURTEENTH CENTURY

In the wake of the minstrels there often came a large troupe of vagrant students and entertainers of all kinds—acrobats, fire-eaters, men leading monkeys and bears, dwarfs, and other freaks of nature.

The smock on the man on the left is slightly fitted with a flare at the bottom. Both men wear hoods pushed behind their necks.

CRAFTSMEN'S WIVES
FRANCE. FOURTEENTH CENTURY

Greek and Roman garments did not distort the human figure, but by the twelfth century a very marked change had taken place, a change which slowly seeped down to the lower classes. On these women we see the "new" style of women's dress—a tightly fitted bodice, lined, interlined, and padded with stiff material, and a long, bell-shaped skirt. The woman on the left is wearing a sleeveless dress of this style over a long, shirtlike undergarment. The long skirt of the other woman's dress is widened by gores in front and back, a typical feature of Gothic costume.

The fantastic Burgundian headgear, with its manifold variety of "horns," was not worn by lower-class women. Traces of its influence can however be found in the hood worn by the woman on the right.

MERCHANTS

FRANCE. FOURTEENTH CENTURY

Each of these merchants seems to think he has gotten the better of the other. Or perhaps the two of them together have outwitted a third.

Only by a wide stretch of our definition of common man can we include these men in the subject of our book. I have drawn them primarily to show what the "other half" was wearing in the fourteenth century.

The Burgundian styles shown here were favored throughout Europe, but especially in France, by people who made any pretense at elegance. The merchant on the left is particularly stylish in his high hat and slightly trailing cloak. Note the puffed sleeves and pleats that begin at the shoulder.

PEASANTS

SPAIN AND FRANCE. FOURTEENTH CENTURY

The improvised festivals celebrated by peasants on the village greens began with picnics, dances, and other frolics, but often ended in bloody fights. The peasant of the Middle Ages was generally inclined to violence and quick to help himself to what he wanted. No wonder, in a period when protection by law scarcely existed and each man's person, family, and property were safe only so far and so long as he was able to help himself.

In this drawing the men, after a generous imbibing of beer or fruit wine (grape wine was reserved for the rich), are about to go after each other with cudgels.

VINTAGERS

GERMANY, FOURTEENTH CENTURY

At harvest time, vineyards were carefully guarded, but needy travelers and pregnant women were permitted to take, free of charge, one handful of grapes at a time. The wine press was usually owned by the lord, and the serf paid him a fee for using it. After fermentation, the wine was preserved by the addition of a small amount of sulphur, as it frequently is today. Spices, honey, and berries were added during the processing, and occasionally also when the wine was served.

Both men and women often wore straw hats when they worked in the open.

BATH HOUSE ATTENDANTS

GERMANY. FOURTEENTH CENTURY

The numerous public baths were open all day except on Sundays and holidays. Hot water and steam were provided, as were barber services and various health treatments. Male and female attendants were employed to soap, massage, and beat the clients with twigs. The attendants formed their own corporation but their morals and hygiene were subject to governmental supervision, frequently to little avail. The reputation of the women, at least, was bad.

The girls in this drawing are clad for work in the hot steam of the bath in simple shifts and hair nets.

DOMESTIC WORKERS
GERMANY, FOURTEENTH CENTURY

Women of a middle class growing in wealth surrounded themselves with maids, cooks, hairdressers, nursemaids, and so on. The hired help took part in all family celebrations and shared their table at meals, but their masters had control over virtually their entire lives. In old age domestic workers were completely dependent on the charity of their employers.

The women in our drawing are dressed for work in long, simple tunics of some coarse material. In contrast to these working clothes, women in this period were already wearing dresses with somewhat fitted and padded bodices and freely flowing skirts.

VAGRANTS

GERMANY. FOURTEENTH CENTURY

Beggary and vagabondage were a perennial concern of medieval authorities, but no laws could suppress or even diminish these activities. These homeless people roamed about roads that were in an indescribably bad condition.

In its better days, the woman's dress undoubtedly belonged to a lady. A fitted bodice and a bell-shaped skirt are still recognizable.

ARTISANS
GERMANY. FOURTEENTH CENTURY

Blacksmiths, weavers, cobblers, and other artisans could still be found in the villages, but the better ones, as well as many landless laborers, tended to drift into towns where they found freedom and a good market for their products. On the other hand, many townspeople also owned and worked on vegetable and fruit gardens, vineyards, and even fields inside and outside of the city walls. As a result, there was scarcely any difference between the rural and urban costumes of the lower classes.

The tunic of the man to the right is in a new style, split all the way down the front and closed by laced buttons. It is on the way to becoming a coat. He is also wearing mittens characteristic of the period. Two of the separate sheaths contain two fingers each; the third one is for the thumb.

SWINEHERD AND SLAUGHTERER
GERMANY. FOURTEENTH CENTURY

The serf driving the pig to its doom wears straight-dropping smock cut like the old Roman tunic, which continues to be the garment most typically worn by the common man at work. Sometimes an old blanket was draped over it.

The slaughterer is wearing something quite different. His coat, which is slit and laced in front, has become tighter, with a padded upper part and a stand-up collar. This fundamental change in man's silhouette developed when the shirtlike, free-hanging coat of chain mail was replaced by armor plate, fitted close to the body. The slaughterer's shoes, with their pointed toes, are another indication that fashions of the upper classes have begun to influence those of the masses.

TOWNSWOMAN AND BEGGAR
ENGLAND. FOURTEENTH CENTURY

The woman on the left, the wife of an artisan or merchant, carefully avoids any contact with the beggar as she drops a coin into her cup. It was a good precaution in an age when contagious diseases were epidemic. More than a third of England's population succumbed to the great bubonic plague, or Black Death, in 1348–49.

One way of distinguishing the classes was by the number of garments a person wore. The townswoman is wearing a dress with a fitted bodice and a skirt pinned up to reveal a long, shirtlike undergarment. A big kerchief covers her shoulders and a smaller one is worn over her head. The beggar's entire costume consists of one very simple dress and one piece of cloth that covers both her head and shoulders.

PEASANTS

ENGLAND. FOURTEENTH CENTURY

Bonded tenants were forced to have their corn ground at the lord's mill, at a monopoly price.

The husband in this drawing is not concerned that his wife is doing the hardest part of the job. Under medieval law and mores, women were virtually without rights and were expected to be the obedient servants of their men. In practice, this was not always the case among the upper classes, but it was with the poor.

STREET MUSICIANS
ENGLAND. FOURTEENTH CENTURY

Large groups of performers, composed of people with a great variety of skills, would play at many events in the nobles' castles and on the squares of towns and villages. Among them were knife-throwers and fire-eaters, and all kinds of acrobats, buffoons, and singers. The most popular were the musicians, like these two fellows, taken from the Luttrell Psalter, who beat the drums or tambourines and played the bagpipes or the flute while people danced.

DOMESTIC SERVANTS

ENGLAND. FOURTEENTH CENTURY

In the kitchen of the lord of the manor an old cook and his assistant are preparing the meal. The cook is using a forklike tool for his work, although forks would not be used for eating until the sixteenth century. A knife and the fingers were made to do, just as they did way back in the days of the Romans. Spoons, on the other hand, actually date back to the Stone Age.

REBELLIOUS PEASANTS
ENGLAND. FOURTEENTH CENTURY

"When Adam delved and Eve span
  Who was then the gentleman?"

With couplets like this, John Ball and other itinerant preachers incited the peasants to join Wat Tyler's Peasants' Revolt of 1381. The revolt culminated in the seizure of the Tower of London, before being bloodily suppressed. Tyler was killed in the aftermath of the fighting and Ball was hanged, drawn, and quartered. With the revolt ended, King Richard II promptly revoked the concessions he had promised Tyler, concessions which would have abolished serfdom. Nevertheless, in the long run, the revolt probably signaled the end of serfdom in England.

Our drawing shows two peasants on the way to join a group of rebels on the march. White crosses are sewn to the fronts of their jerkins. They are armed with big swords and any equipment they could get hold of.

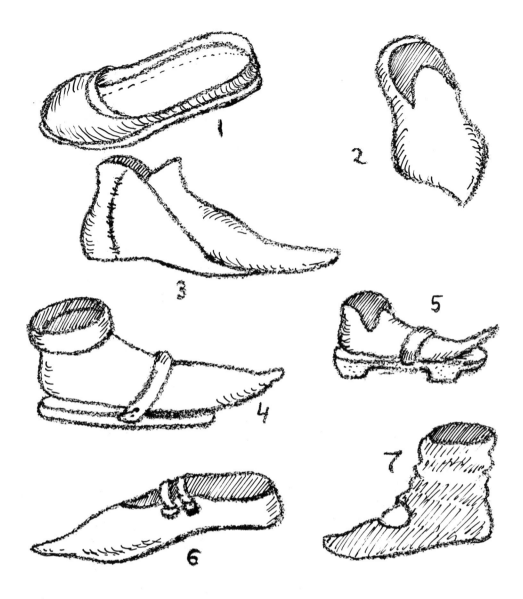

SHOES OF THE LOWER CLASSES
ELEVENTH TO FOURTEENTH CENTURIES

The slippers (1 and 2) and the stocking boot (7) are peasant shoes, worn by both men and women. They were also worn by lower-class townspeople all through the Middle Ages.

The shoes with the long, pointed toes (3, 4, 5, and 6) were variously called poulaine, Pigaschen, and Schnabelschuhe. They first made their appearance in the eleventh century, almost disappeared during the twelfth century, but enjoyed a triumphant comeback at the beginning of the thirteenth century. By the end of the fourteenth century, they had completely disappeared. These shoes, worn by both sexes and by all classes of people, were usually, although not exclusively, used by those living in towns. The pointed shoes of the lower classes never reached the extravagant lengths of those worn by upper-class people.

Pattens (4 and 5) were sometimes strapped beneath these heelless shoes whose thin soles were little suited to street conditions.

Fifteenth Century

CARRIER AND TOWNSWOMAN
SPAIN. FIFTEENTH CENTURY

The carrier is dressed with a certain dashing elegance, which we often find with men in his occupation, right up to the romantic postilion of the eighteenth century. The carrier's trade made him welcome with everyone along his route, and typically it was said that he had a girl in every town.

His outfit has a strong regional Spanish flavor.

According to my source for the woman's costume, the Book of Hours of Queen Isabella, the townswoman's dress would have been very colorful—a green hood on top of a white head covering; a long-sleeved red dress over a green undergarment, with an orange-yellow skirt beneath it all.

JUGGLERS

SPAIN. FIFTEENTH CENTURY

Wandering jugglers, jesters, and other show people were held in low esteem. Crowds of them, along with beggars and other adventurers, could be found in Madrid and in the smaller towns too. Strolling comedians even gave shows in the villages, if they were not too far off the main road.

In Spain, as in France where many a jongleur was hired to recite his master's verses in public, the borderline between juggler and musician was a blurred one. Jugglers often doubled as singers while musicians, in a pinch, might also juggle.

SOLDIERS
SWITZERLAND. FIFTEENTH CENTURY

In each town, citizens formed their own militia to settle disputes with neighboring towns and to fight off the bands of robber barons and outlaws.

Although the marksman's doublet (1) is modern, he is still wearing the old shoe with extremely elongated toes. The other soldier (2) has on the new duckbill shoe introduced by the lansquenets, mercenary Swiss and German soldiers who served in foreign countries.

BEGGING MUSICIANS
ITALY, EARLY FIFTEENTH CENTURY

War refugees of every sort swelled the ranks of the beggars who roamed through the country in the fifteenth century. Demobilized soldiers joined up with the bands of ingrained idlers and vagrants. So, too, did the peasants and townspeople who had lost their possessions in the destruction wrought by Italy's small, innumerable regional wars. Changing labor conditions also pushed many workers into the low and insecure class of the unorganized, adding to the number of itinerant beggars.

SHEPHERDS

FRANCE. 1400–1450

The shepherd's flock was kept in the open and at night was usually gathered in to the same fold that the shepherd slept in too. In general, there was no essential difference between the dwellings of a peasant and his animals. Both lived, usually together, in a cabin or shack made of wood, clay, and straw. The shepherd's favorite pastime was music, which he performed on such instruments as horns, bagpipes, pipes, flageolets, or shawms.

The tunics worn by both men, like many peasant clothes, are probably made of ticking. The shepherd on the left is wearing a sheepskin as a kind of apron.

INVALID SOLDIERS
FRANCE. FIFTEENTH CENTURY

The lot of a soldier wounded in one of the many wars of the fifteenth century was indeed a miserable one. His physical disability, along with the bad reputation soldiers generally had, barred him from any legitimate profession. So, if he was fit enough, he became a robber; if he was disabled, a beggar.

DYERS

FRANCE. FIFTEENTH CENTURY

Dyers formed a guild, or corps de metier, of their own. Each guild held a monopoly over its particular branch of work, and set strict rules for entrance into the guild. Independent workers were reluctantly tolerated only in certain vaguely defined professions or, on occasion, as itinerant workmen. However, in the larger cities of France in the late Middle Ages, the guilds were beginning to lose their grip over their craft, and in some professions any competent craftsman was permitted to open shop, subject only to government regulations.

The sleeveless doublet of the dyer on the right, with its buttoned front and tiny skirt, is the forerunner of the waistcoat.

LAUNDRESSES

FRANCE. FIFTEENTH CENTURY

The woman on the left cannot afford the services of the laundress, right, and must do her own washing. She will use ash-lye to get her clothes clean.

My sources for the costumes in this drawing were the Hours of Louis de Savoie and an early French copy of Boccaccio's *Decameron*. The illustrators depicted the working garments worn by lower-class women in shades of blues and grayish purples. Both of these women have tucked up their outer skirts before getting to work.

CRAFTSMAN AND WIFE

FRANCE. FIFTEENTH CENTURY

Although the master has somehow displeased his wife, he seems to be taking her reaction with equanimity.

The woman is quite stylish. Her stiffened hood is related to the fashionable lady's henin, and her dress, with its tightly fitted bodice and gored skirt cut in one piece, shows the Burgundian influence. The husband, on the other hand, is dressed in the old-fashioned manner. His simple smock is of an undyed material, his hood with its long liripipe is red, and his stockings are blue. The wife's hood is red, and her other garments are in the blues and purplish reds that were popular in the fifteenth century.

INN SERVANT AND TRAVELER
ENGLAND. EARLY FIFTEENTH CENTURY

Although by the fifteenth century there were many inns along the roads of England, most of them were of doubtful quality. Separate rooms were available only to the well-to-do. All others had to share one common room.

The servant woman is barefoot, as most people of her class were when they were indoors. Her head, however, is carefully wrapped against the cold, which permeated the whole inn. The stiffened square on top of her head cloths serves to support heavy loads. The bag the traveler is carrying is undoubtedly all the luggage he has. It doesn't seem like much, even for a poor man, but in the Middle Ages most people could travel only on foot and carry their baggage themselves.

PRISONER AND JAILER
ENGLAND. EARLY FIFTEENTH CENTURY

Prisons in the foulest possible conditions were always filled to capacity. Nor were the inmates by any means all criminals. In this period of continuous civil strife, the jails were always full of religious and political dissenters.

At a time when not much entertainment was available to the common man, the parading and torturing of minor offenders provided a spectacle only second in popularity to public capital punishment.

The poor soul in this drawing, after a law treatise of the reign of Henry VI, is being led either to trial or to punishment. His belt has been taken away and his long hair and beard prove that, whatever his fate, he has been awaiting it in jail for a long time.

GLASS BLOWERS
ENGLAND. EARLY FIFTEENTH CFNTURY

The Romans introduced the use and manufacture of glass to the provinces of Italy. After the Dark Ages, the first revival of glassmaking took place in the monasteries. When the Venetians conquered Constantinople in 1204, they brought back examples of the marvelous Byzantine glass and inspired their own glass industry to its highest achievements. From Venice, glassmaking spread throughout the continent and then to England, where it was to find its real development in Elizabethan days.

BUILDING WORKERS

ENGLAND. 1400–1450

The most grandiose and impressive memorials the Middle Ages have left us are the Romanesque and Gothic cathedrals to be seen all over Europe. Our drawing shows two members of the building craft engaged in this monumental work. While most crafts- men belonged to guilds, which regulated their per- sonal, as well as professional, lives, builders belonged to unions. In many respects, these unions were similar to those we have today.

The hat on the laborer to the left has a long his- tory. It is a further development of the old capuchon, which was first pulled up and then built into a com- plicated turban, and was sometimes inserted into a separate roll around the head.

TRAVELERS

ITALY. MID-FIFTEENTH CENTURY

Much of our knowledge of the way common people dressed in this century we owe to the fact that biblical stories were a major source of inspiration for medieval artists, who painted their subjects in contemporary dress. Thus, as the presence of shepherds at the Nativity showed us how medieval shepherds looked, the flight of the Holy Family to Egypt tells us what ordinary people in the fifteenth century wore when traveling on the roads.

A popular garment with people of some means was the overcoat worn by the man in this drawing, with wide, three-quarter-length sleeves.

SAILORS

FLANDERS. MID-FIFTEENTH CENTURY

By the mid-century big commercial houses, like the
Medici in Italy and others in Flanders, France, and
Germany, were in full bloom. Large commercial fleets
left all the bigger European ports, sailing in all directions to the most remote countries. The smocks on
these two sailors were depicted in reddish brown.
Their hose was blue and their shoes brown.

BOATMEN
GERMANY. MID-FIFTEENTH CENTURY

Roads were indescribably bad and, for the most part, very unsafe. Rich people went about on horseback or in rather clumsy horsedrawn vehicles, but everyone else travelled on foot. After a long period of rain, the mire came up to the knees or even higher, sometimes making further passage impossible. Except in some places, where the remnants of old Roman roads still existed, very few roads were built on rock foundations. Good, solid bridges were rare and one had to rely on the often irregular services of barges.

Because of the unsafe condition of the roads, rivers were the most important, and often the only, means of transportation for men and goods. Skilled skippers and sailors, like these two in our drawing, were in great demand. For their hard work, both men are wearing simple tunics. In summer they would not be wearing their tight stockings.

70

MARKET WOMEN

GERMANY. MID-FIFTEENTH CENTURY

The townsman looks with a suspicious eye at the produce offered by the peasant women. Although there was not yet a very clear distinction between the clothes worn by town and country people, their hoods and simple, loose smocks mark these women as peasants. (A peasant woman might also wrap a kerchief around her head, as would a townswoman of the lower classes.) Not until the sixteenth century would there be a very distinct differentiation between the clothes worn in the towns and those worn by peasants.

The vegetables used in German cooking were mainly peas, lentils, and cabbage. Some beets, carrots, and lettuce were brought to market, too.

TRAMP AND TOWNSWOMAN
GERMANY. MID-FIFTEENTH CENTURY

The tramp is good-natured but determined. Obviously he has no intention of returning the stolen goose.

The woman's dress, with its sleeves buttoned to it at the armhole, indicates that she is probably a townswoman rather than a peasant. Except for her face, her head is completely veiled, with a gorget, or wimple, wrapped around her neck and chin. A kerchief floating in the wind is held on her head by a small round cap.

MARKET WOMAN AND CUSTOMER

GERMANY. MID-FIFTEENTH CENTURY

The market woman, right, is dressed more fashionably than her customer, who is wearing a simple tunic in the style that lower-class women have been wearing for almost a century. Quite probably this market woman was a townswoman rather than a peasant. Many artisans also had vegetable and fruit gardens in town, and their wives made a little extra money selling the produce on the market.

VAGRANTS

GERMANY. MID-FIFTEENTH CENTURY

Vagabondage, beggary, and street robbery were common throughout the Middle Ages, no matter how many laws were passed to control them. Moreover, with constant political and religious strife, the reservoir of outcasts was always being replenished. For example, after the big peasant uprising in the sixteenth century, one provincial government would order that, in each town, sixty of the citizens who joined the rebels be blinded and driven into the streets.

German beggars and vagabonds, like the French, belonged to highly organized guilds that were ruled by beggar kings.

PEASANTS IN WINTER
FRANCE. MID-FIFTEENTH CENTURY

These two peasants are making rather futile attempts at getting a little warmth from their fireplace. Although some houses in Germany and France were equipped with chimneys, in many others the fire was lit in the middle of the main room, with the smoke allowed to escape through a gap in the roof, which could be closed with a wooden lid.

Rooms were dark, drafty, and when the fire was lit, filled with smoke. To preserve the warmth, all openings except for the door were closed by wooden shutters or stuffed with hay. The windows were covered with oiled parchment or paper.

PEASANTS AT A SPRING DANCE

FRANCE. MID-FIFTEENTH CENTURY

We can only really appreciate the impact of the coming of spring on people of the Middle Ages if we try to imagine the interminable hours of a long winter spent in their poorly heated and lighted houses.

The two youngsters here are enjoying the first open-air dance of the year. The boy, who may be rushing the season, is already dressed for warm weather in a sleeveless doublet over a shirt with rolled-up sleeves. His short, footless leggings are carelessly laced to the doublet.

The maiden's dress is both warmer and more modest. Her head is completely covered by a chaperon with a liripipe. She wears a long-sleeved long undergarment below her short-sleeved dress with its tucked-up skirt.

DRUNKEN PEASANT AND WIFE

FRANCE. MID-FIFTEENTH CENTURY

This peasant has had himself too good a time, and now his wife is trying to prevent him from making a lot of noise in places where he shouldn't. During periods when the living conditions were comparatively good, rustic fairs and weddings were celebrated with music and dances, but most of all—and this was typical throughout the Middle Ages—with an enormous amount of eating and drinking. Beer was the usual drink; hard liquor was drunk only occasionally.

The tight-fitting doublet which we saw on the Swiss marksman (see page 57) was poorly designed for the average peasant, since it hampered movement and was easily worn out. Many peasants preferred this wider, more comfortable version of the doublet.

PEASANT WOMEN
FRANCE. MID-FIFTEENTH CENTURY

By the middle of the fifteenth century, the Burgundian silhouette had been adopted by country people as well as the more sophisticated city dwellers. These women, walking to their harvest chores, are wearing tight bodices, and skirts that have been widened by gores.

Unlike their clothes, however, agricultural techniques and tools have remained the same through the centuries. The women in our drawing are carrying a wooden fork and rake.

PEASANTS
FRANCE. MID-FIFTEENTH CENTURY

While most of the harvesting was done with a sickle, hay was cut with a scythe. The whetstone used to sharpen it was carried in a case strapped to the reaper's belt. Some illustrations in prayerbooks depict the stockings and smocks as made from unbleached, coarse linen. Others show hues of pink or blue. The shoes would be black leather.

WIDOW AND BUTCHER

FRANCE. MID-FIFTEENTH CENTURY

Butchering animals for human consumption was a trade strictly regulated by both governmental regulations and the rules of the butchers' guild. Under medieval "pure food" laws, it was forbidden to sell goat for lamb, or still-born calves for milk calves. Butchers were also forbidden to color the meat or put a thumb on the scale. The constant reiteration of these rules makes it apparent that they were not necessarily obeyed.

The woman customer is wearing a widow's bonnet. Her apron, typical of that worn by working women, is a rectangular piece of linen decorated with simple embroidery.

PEASANTS
FRANCE. MID-FIFTEENTH CENTURY

Although by now peasants owned some of the land, they remained dependent in many ways on the seigneur. They were still heavily burdened by an enormous number of taxes under a variety of names; the tax collector sometimes even took their pots and pans. There were, however, great differences in the condition of the peasants according to the amount of land they possessed, with the landless laborer at the bottom of the heap. In general, peasants lived on potatoes and rye bread. Their only meat might be a little bacon or the entrails and heads of the animals, with the rest of the meat going to the nobles.

EXECUTIONERS

FRANCE. MID-FIFTEENTH CENTURY

Hangmen, like gravediggers, street sweepers, barbers, and chimney sweeps, were held in ill repute. Still, with death a most common punishment for lawbreaking, the hangman was a person very much in demand. Even twelve-year-old children were known to be hanged for minor thefts. Murderers and robbers of low rank were twisted to the wheel. Noblemen were beheaded. Witches, sorcerers, heretics, arsonists, sodomists, and homosexuals were burned.

Both executioners wear short breeches. The man on the right has drawn a pair of leggings over them, but has strapped the cord that holds them up at the waist rather carelessly. To judge from contemporary drawings, this slothfulness was not uncommon among the lower classes.

HUNTERS

GERMANY, LATE FIFTEENTH CENTURY

The hunt known as battue was a favorite pastime among nobles of all countries. The game was first scared out by beaters and then chased by the hounds and hunters until it was brought to bay and killed by lances or arrows. In form, we can see, the sport has changed very little in five hundred years.

The man on the left, blowing a little horn and holding a dog's leash, is in charge of the hounds. His companion is one of the beaters.

PEASANTS
GERMANY. LATE FIFTEENTH CENTURY

The peasant's coat, as worn by the man in this drawing, was an important sartorial development of the Middle Ages. Out of it would come the justau-corps of the seventeenth and eighteenth centuries, which, in turn, would become the modern man's coat.

The evolution of the coat began when the working man's smock was split all the way down the front, and then put on from the back. The peasant's coat was cut straight, with no waistline. What appears in this drawing to be a flared skirt is actually nothing but the effect of a cord tied around the waist. The coat had wide sleeves and, in general, was such a comfortable garment that it was soon adopted by craftsmen and other common people in the towns as well as the country.

The woman is wearing a gorget, or wimple, under her hood. See also the drawing on page 72.

84

TRAVELER IN AN INN
GERMANY. LATE FIFTEENTH CENTURY

Despite the bad road conditions and the ever-present danger of being set upon by robbers, the highways were crowded with travelers—pilgrims and beggar monks, vagrant students and artisans, messengers and unemployed lansquenets. Peasants and peddlers rode in carts; merchants rode in carriages.

Our traveler is leaving the inn, and a sullen servant hands him his filled canteen. We may be sure he departs with little regret, since inns had a deservedly bad reputation. The arriving traveler was greeted with neither a welcoming word nor gesture. He entered into a common room in which people changed their shirts, dried their clothes, and washed in a communal tub filled with dirty water. In the same room was the common table where the guests sat down to eat and drink.

French and English inns were considered somewhat better than those of Spain or Germany.

SAILORS

FRANCE. LATE FIFTEENTH CENTURY

The two sailors on shore leave are out for some fun. Except, perhaps, for the hat worn by the man on the left, their clothes are not distinguishable from those of any other working man. Both wear the usual, leggings, tied to a cord around the waist and closed in front by a flap. The man on the left wears a shirt-like tunic, the other a doublet buttoned at the neck and fastened down the front with hooks.

BEGGARS

FRANCE. LATE FIFTEENTH CENTURY

The number of beggars in France, as in all of the European countries, was enormous. At one time during the fifteenth century, there were an estimated 80,000 beggars in Paris alone, where they formed their own kingdom under their own powerful king.

Large bands of beggars operated in the provinces too, where the most notorious band was the Coquillards of the Bourgogne. Like the guilds of the Middle Ages, beggar bands were organized into groups of apprentices, journeymen, and masters. To achieve the master's degree, a beggar had to perform a masterpiece, such as cutting a woman's pouch during a church service without being observed.

BEGGARS
FRANCE. LATE FIFTEENTH CENTURY

The fifteenth century produced a rich literature about professional beggars and vagabonds. The most notable were the ballads of François Villon, the sermons of Geiler and Kaiserberg, and Brant's allegorical satire *Ship of Fools*. The most definitive work was *Liber Vagatorum*, published between 1494 and 1499, which dealt with twenty-eight groups of robbers and pickpockets, cardsharps, beggars, tramps, and the like.

VINTAGERS
BURGUNDY. LATE FIFTEENTH CENTURY

The vintager worked a thirteen-hour day, from five in the morning until six at night. Moreover, if he did not keep strictly to these hours, he lost an entire day's pay, which at best was barely enough to cover his necessities.

The construction of men's trousers evolved during the Middle Ages from a pair of separate leggings, as worn by these two men, to a single pair of pants.

Heretofore, the leggings were drawn up over a short pair of breeches and then held up by a belt around the waist. Sometimes, as in this drawing, the leggings were tied to a tunic or doublet. In the second half of the fifteenth century, some ingenious soul joined the two legs by means of a gore at the back and a flap in front.

BEGGARS

ITALY. LATE FIFTEENTH CENTURY

The dress of the very poor often amounted to nothing but layers of rags—hand-me-downs or remnants that were found or stolen, or even taken from graves.

The sores or mutilations exhibited by many beggars were possibly real, but just as possibly false. Small children were known to have been kidnapped, crippled, and then used to beg.

WOOD CARVER AND TOWNSWOMAN
ITALY. LATE FIFTEENTH CENTURY

The artisan has set himself up in the market, where he carves his spoons and sells them at the same time. The customer looks over each spoon carefully, since the time has not yet come when products are turned out completely alike.

Scenes like this one may still be observed in Italy, especially at the weekly markets in the small towns, where the crowd is still as spirited and vivacious as it was in the time of our drawing. Of course, the native costumes and the hand-made crafts have been replaced almost entirely by mass-produced goods.

Notice particularly the woman's headdress. A small board inserted under the kerchief above the forehead forms the angular plane. This fashion will survive in Italy for many years to come.

PEASANTS

UPPER ITALY. LATE FIFTEENTH CENTURY

The woman is on her way to market to sell the produce from her small farm. Writers of the quattrocento sang the praises of the gardeners who provided much of the daily food for people in both cities and towns. The most popular crops were spinach, onions, turnips, cabbage, and olives. Neither potatoes or tomatoes were known.

The man is wearing short breeches with no leggings over them, a form of dress that townspeople, even those of the lower classes, considered thoroughly disreputable. In fact, the appearance of this couple seems illustrative of the story of a Tuscan peasant who always slept in the stable because he was afraid somebody might steal his animals, but felt sure no one would carry off his wife.

PHYSICIAN AND TOWNSMAN
FLANDERS, LATE FIFTEENTH CENTURY

The most famous medical schools of the Middle Ages were located at Montpelier and Salerno. Only the graduate of a medical school was entitled to wear the doctor's long robe like the practitioner in this drawing, who examines a patient's urine to determine what ails him. Just as urine examination was the primary diagnostic tool, so bloodletting was the most general form of treatment. Of course, not all of those who practiced medicine were graduate doctors, and men with no training at all often performed fearful operations or prescribed such horrid brews as mixtures of scorpion oil and ant eggs.

The life expectancy of a man in the Middle Ages was short. Polluted water and generally filthy living conditions made all Europe the host of epidemics, the most notorious of which was the great Black Death, commonly believed to have been the bubonic plague.

WOMEN AT WORK

GERMANY. END OF FIFTEENTH CENTURY

When an artist of this era wanted to depict a peasant woman, he generally showed her wearing a hat. Women generally did not wear hats, and lower-class women never wore them except when working in the fields.

Of course, the fact that the woman at left is holding a rake also makes it obvious that she is a peasant, not a townswoman. Her dress, with its typical Gothic godets, is tucked up to reveal her petticoat.

The head of the townswoman is completely veiled in two kerchiefs. She is wearing a version of the double apron, which we will see again in the sixteenth century.

TOWNSFOLK IN WINTER

FRANCE. END OF FIFTEENTH CENTURY

The very long smock, as worn by the man in this drawing, was a favorite garment of older people. Even though he is indoors, he wears a cape with a fur-lined collar over it, and a hat. The woman, too, has left her head wrapped up and is wearing her fur hat.

Precautions like these prove that even in the towns, houses were poorly heated, or at best heated in only a few rooms. This despite the fact that some houses had stoves or fireplaces or both. Wood was the most common fuel, although coal was in use as early as the eleventh century. Windows were kept closed all winter and light was provided by tallow candles, or by fat or whale oil lit in lamps.

SAILORS

SPAIN. END OF FIFTEENTH CENTURY

These were the great days of the Spanish marine. Following the voyages of Columbus and the Spanish explorers, fleets of as many as several dozens of merchant ships, protected by battleships, commuted twice a year between Seville and Mexico and Panama.

In this drawing, the sailor on the right is wearing a very simple, comfortably wide smock that was especially suitable for the hard work at sea.

HOST AND SERVANT IN AN INN

SPAIN. END OF FIFTEENTH CENTURY

If this innkeeper and his waiter look more like vagabonds than citizens of good repute, it is because we
have followed the descriptions of contemporary literature. In Spain, innkeepers were the social equals of
street walkers, pimps, gypsies, Moors, and show people.

As noted before, the inns of the Middle Ages were
the worst kinds of flophouses. The man or woman
who poured the wine, from a goat- or pig-skin, was
dirty and dressed in rags. The fire which was lit in
the center of the kitchen spewed its smoke throughout
the building, since there was no proper chimney or
other escape. The straw to which one retired to sleep
teemed with bedbugs—by the time guests rose in the
morning, their faces might be completely unrecognizable as a result of the bites.

SAILORS

ENGLAND. END OF FIFTEENTH CENTURY

By the fourteenth century, the English merchant marine was already engaged in sea-going commerce. Under the command of a royal admiral, it had also fought successfully in the wars between England and France.

But now, by the end of the fifteenth century, the merchant marine really came of age. Its ships, with two or three masts, were much better equipped, with comfortable accommodations for passengers and even cabins for the crews.

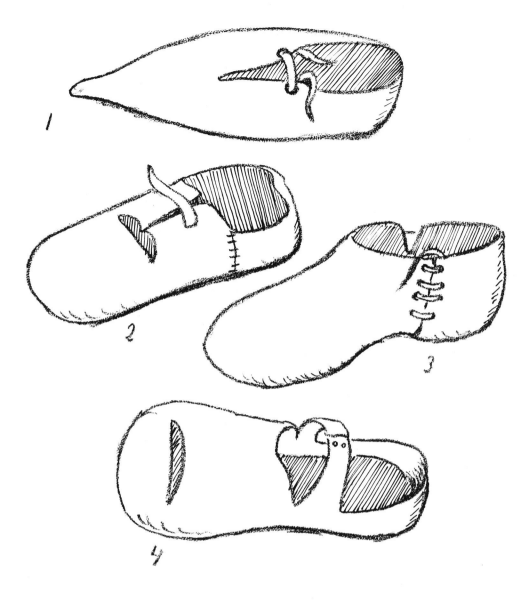

SHOES OF THE LOWER CLASSES

FIFTEENTH AND SIXTEENTH CENTURIES

1. Black leather, laced across the front. This shoe, typical of those worn by the common man in the fifteenth century, is a remnant of the medieval style. At the end of the century, it was replaced by the blunt-toed German shoe.

2. A construction of the early sixteenth century. The upper part of the shoe is made in two sections, with the heel stiffened from the inside. The sole consists of an inner sole, the welt, and the outer sole. The shoes were usually made of black or gray leather.

They were still without heels, which did not come into style until the end of the sixteenth century.

3. Black leather. Early sixteenth century. Fastened at the side in the medieval fashion.

4. Black leather duckbill, or German-type, shoe, which became popular around 1540. The upper part was made of thick hide, cut low at the back. The shoe had a single sole.

The drawings on this page were taken from an exhibit of shoes in the London Museum, 1961.

88988

Sixteenth Century

WOMEN'S HEADGEAR
NETHERLANDS, SIXTEENTH CENTURY

These are a few of the many varieties of headcoverings worn by women in the Netherlands in the sixteenth century.

The women in figures 1, 3, and 4 are wearing stiffened kerchiefs, cut and ironed to shape, and generally white. Figure 2 shows a small linen cap with a kerchief of light material tied around head and chin.

The woman who worked in the fields might, as in figure 5, put a hat on over a kerchief.

Women often wore a brimless, bowl-shaped hat (figure 6), similar to those worn by men. The small cap (figure 7) on the young girl was formed from a soft kerchief.

STREET VENDORS
PARIS. SIXTEENTH CENTURY

According to *Cris de Paris*, a book of drawings depicting the lives of people of the city, there were one hundred thirty-six itinerant merchants in Paris at one time during the century. They sold all kinds of food, as well as a great variety of other portable wares.

The man in the drawing is selling cakes; the woman, fish. Their costume, especially that of the man, has a somewhat old-fashioned look about it compared to the clothes worn by the two vendors in the next drawing.

STREET VENDORS

PARIS. SIXTEENTH CENTURY

In the whole of Paris there were no more than sixteen fountains with drinkable water. As a result, the vendor who had a drink to sell could make a good bit of money. Quite possibly, the liquid in this vendor's bottle is not just water.

Street vendors played an important role in the commercial life of Paris in the sixteenth century. Among the many items they sold were pictures, pamphlets, and popular books. Their ranks also included itinerant artisans—glaciers, chimney sweeps, joiners, and the like. All of the vendors offered their wares at the tops of their voices. Sometimes they chanted traditional ditties or accompanied their calls with ringing bells or rattles.

PEASANT AND SAILOR
PORTUGAL. EARLY SIXTEENTH CENTURY

During the reign of King Manuel I (1495–1521), the explorations of such daring seafarers as Vasco da Gama and Pedro Alvares Cabral helped make Portugal one of Europe's leading sea powers, outranking even Venice.

Clearly, the peasant has never seen anything like the pineapple which the old salt has brought back from one of those great trips of discovery. The beret on the sailor is slashed in the German manner. The rest of his costume is the one worn by the lower classes throughout Europe in the fifteenth century. The peasant's outfit, on the other hand, shows early Portuguese elements. Even today, his unbleached linen smock and flat black hat can be seen on fishermen of Algarve, Minho, and other provinces.

STOCKYARD WORKERS

BARCELONA. SIXTEENTH CENTURY

Short breeches, as seen on these two men pulling a heavy barge, were generally worn under long leggings. Catalans were considered the most industrious workers of Spain, resembling in that respect the French, many of whom also worked in Barcelona.

The source for this and the following drawing is the *Trachtenbuch* by Christoph Weiditz, a young German goldsmith, who was sent to Spain by his employers to deliver a suit of armor; on his way he did a series of sketches of the people he met. These sketches are an almost unique source for the popular dress of many regions.

WATER VENDORS

BARCELONA, EARLY SIXTEENTH CENTURY

Since Spaniards despised and avoided all "vile" occupations, it is safe to assume that these water carriers were foreigners. Many other craftsmen who worked in Spain—masons, carpenters, tailors, and the like—were foreigners too, and they earned much more money in Spain than they would have at home.

The short, sleeveless cloak, open at the sides, was a popular garment with working men all over Europe. In this drawing, only the wide, stuffed breeches worn by the man on the right are typically Spanish. They are probably of Arab origin.

SOLDIERS

GERMANY. CIRCA 1500

The German Empire was divided into a great many principalities and territories. The princes, dukes, counts, margraves, barons, and bishops who ruled these domains did so completely independently of the Emperor. They were the real masters of their own inhabitants. Each of them maintained his own army, and although uniforms in the modern sense did not exist before the second half of the seventeenth century, there was a certain uniformity in the armament and dress of a particular ruler's men.

PEASANT AND BLACKSMITH

GERMANY. CIRCA 1500

The peasant appears dubious about the knife he has just purchased from the blacksmith.

Within the towns, the organization of the guilds resulted in considerable specialization and separation of tasks. Among metal-workers alone, there were armorers, cutlers, goldsmiths, blacksmiths, scythe makers, and so on.

In the villages, on the other hand, the smithy per-formed a wide variety of jobs. He was a person held in high esteem, even in the days when he was still a serf, and he and his workshops enjoyed special privi-leges and protection.

The coat worn by the peasant in this drawing is in the new style, cut all the way down the front. Here it was sleeveless, but with or without sleeves, this was the beginning of the modern man's coat.

110

TOWNSWOMEN AT A MARKET

GERMANY. CIRCA 1500

As yet, there was no real distinction between the dress worn by the common people who lived in town and those who lived in the country. Both of these townswomen, like the peasants in the drawings on page 117, are wearing the double apron. The front and back bibs were held together at the shoulders with ribbons; these could be loosened to let the bibs drop.

At the turn of the century, a new garment was added to the female costume, a small shoulder cape, called a Koller or Goller in German, a collet in France. The capes, worn by both of the women in this drawing, were made of sturdy linen or wool. They were circular and hooked either just at the neck or all the way down the front.

COOPERS

GERMANY. CIRCA 1500

According to Hans Sachs of Nuremberg, a shoe-maker and poet immortalized by Wagner in his *Meistersinger*, the cooper made "with pride out of pine, fir, and oakwood, tubes, pails, buckets, vats, and coops as well as wine and beer casks."

Like the other artisans' guilds, the coopers' guild played a role in the city government, regulating the standards of both producers and products. The guilds made sure that all of their members used the same tools and materials. For instance, a craftsman might be forbidden to use a turning-wheel because it would facilitate his work too much and give him an advantage over his competitors.

The source for these costumes is the Krakauer Behaim Codex, a collection of material dealing with city government, compiled in Krakau, Poland, in 1505. Krakau, at that time, was inhabited almost exclusively by Germans. The codex contains a section on craftsmen and their guilds, illustrated with beautiful miniatures.

JOINERS
GERMANY. CIRCA 1500

The rules promulgated by the guilds went so far as to stipulate the manner in which their members should dress. For example, "The artisan should dress discreetly and not ostentatiously." Apparently, the trousers worn by the man on the left, which are made of differently colored sections of material, were considered sufficiently unostentatious and discreet.

Outside of the house, unless he was at work, the artisan was expected to show his respectability by wearing a hat, a cloak and collar, and gloves. Even the forms of conventional greetings and the manner of addressing persons of higher rank were prescribed.

BAKERS

GERMANY. CIRCA 1500

As they are working close to the oven, both men have taken off their coats and tied them around their waists, thus giving us a good idea of what the shirts worn by laborers looked like. (Other contemporary illustrators, including Jost Amman, show bakers working completely naked, except for a loin cloth.) The round, white bonnets were the mark of cooks and bakers.

Guild and government regulations for the weight, price, and quality of a product were especially strict in all countries for bakers. In France, for example, bakers were forbidden to use an excess of yeast to blow up the size of their loaves and sell "bubbles of air" instead of bread. In Nuremberg, bakers were allowed to sell only rye bread in the market, with the finer breads restricted to certain other locations. In Nuremberg, too, we find a report of a baker who had both of his ears cut off (and one of his wife's) because his loaves were too small.

TOWNSWOMAN AND PROSTITUTE
SWITZERLAND. EARLY SIXTEENTH CENTURY

Each in her own way, the harlot and the towns-woman express contempt for the other. Prostitution was recognized as a necessary evil and was regulated, even encouraged, by the authorities. This permissive attitude was gradually to change until, in 1609, follow-ing the lead of some local governments, Switzerland passed laws expelling prostitutes from its borders.

Prostitutes had to display the mark of their trade in their dress. In Zurich and Bern, they wore red bonnets and, later, green skirts.

PEASANTS

SWITZERLAND. EARLY SIXTEENTH CENTURY

Here we see a sleeved variety of the coat worn by the man in the drawing on page 110. This type of peasant coat was probably the most important contribution of the common man to general costume. While new fashions typically originated with the upper classes and filtered down, with simplifications and omissions, to the masses, the history of the man's coat is just the reverse. It started with the peasant coat, later became the coat worn by soldiers in the Thirty Years War, then the justaucorps, and, finally, the coat still worn by men today.

PEASANT WOMEN
FLANDERS, EARLY SIXTEENTH CENTURY

The typical costume of the peasant woman in the sixteenth century was a one-piece, ankle-length belted dress worn over a long-sleeved shirt. An apron and a pair of coarse leather shoes completed the outfit.

Both women here are wearing the double apron we saw on pages 94 and 111. The woman on the left is wearing the typical peasant's shoe, or Bundschuh, which became the symbol of suppressed peasantry in the great rebellion of 1524.

PEASANTS
ENGLAND AND FLANDERS. EARLY SIXTEENTH CENTURY

Much of what we know of the daily life and appearance of the peasants of this era we have learned from the beautiful miniatures that illustrate the prayer-books (or books of hours) of the great. The attire worn by our peasants, for example, came from the Great Book of Hours of Henry VIII and a Flemish calendar of the early sixteenth century. A favorite theme of miniaturists was "the labors of the month."

The illustrations for these works, done in loving detail, are much more informative and revealing than the contemporary literature, which generally dealt with peasants simply by denouncing their crudity, savagery, cunning, and avarice.

PEASANTS

NETHERLANDS. EARLY SIXTEENTH CENTURY

Lucas van Leyden, whose engravings of peasants are the source for the costumes in this drawing, was one of the artists whose work gives an insight into the appearance of ordinary people in the Renaissance. Supposedly, some of his engravings were published when he was only nine years old, but fourteen is probably more accurate. In the centuries to come, his peasants, in varying situations in life, would be models for all the masters of genre painting, including Brueghel, Ostade, Brouwer, and Le Nain.

SLAUGHTERER

FRANCE. EARLY SIXTEENTH CENTURY

This slaughterer might have been working in a shop, assisted by a woman servant. But he also might have been called to a farm—at certain times of the year, he might have made the rounds of several farms—to do all the slaughtering and processing of meat, with the help of the woman of the house. Since the big season for slaughtering was in the late fall, we frequently find illustrations of such work used to represent that season of the year.

CARPENTERS
GERMANY. EARLY SIXTEENTH CENTURY

In general, craftsmen worked an average of twelve to fifteen hours a day. In most trades, the working day was longer in summer than in winter. Although night work was forbidden in some professions, in others it was the rule. These very long working hours were partly compensated for by the great number of holidays—so many, indeed, that sometimes workers protested the number because of loss of income. (Obviously, holidays with pay were not part of the work picture.) Sundays and Mondays were the usual days off, and in addition to many religious holidays, there would be one free day for the funeral of a guild member and another when mass was read for his soul. Work was halted to celebrate the birthday of the master craftsman or a member of his family, the entry of a prince into the town, or some other similar occasion.

PEASANT AND LANSQUENET

GERMANY. 1520–1530

Except in England, where serfdom virtually died out in the fifteenth century, the peasant's burden worsened as the power and privileges of the nobility, the towns, and the clergy grew stronger. His duties and obligations seemed endless. He was not only suppressed and exploited, but held in deep contempt, a clumsy, filthy, and incredibly ugly target of jokes. According to the description of a Swiss prebendary, he was "a man with his back bent like a mountain, dirty face, bleary eyes beneath bristly eyebrows, a mighty goiter, torn and soiled clothes, exposing the shaggy skin of an animal." One of the hardest plights the much-suffering peasant had to bear was the ever-recurring looting, murder, rape, and arson carried out by his lord's enemies, or even by his lord's own soldiers.

REBELLIOUS PEASANTS

GERMANY. 1524

In 1524, when the peasants finally rebelled, it was with a violence no one apparently had anticipated. Not that there hadn't been storm warnings before. Peasant uprisings had occurred throughout the Middle Ages—for instance, in Flanders in 1323; the revolt of the Jacquerie in France in 1358; and, only a few years before the great uprising, the movement of the Arme Conrad (poor Conrad) in Suevia. But the great peasant rebellion of 1524–25 was the largest revolutionary outbreak in Europe before the French Revolution.

Both of the men in this drawing are wearing characteristic peasant costume, long, tight leggings and the typical peasant coat. The man on the left is wearing the Bundschuh that was the symbol of the rebellion. His companion is wearing the old stocking boot.

REBELLIOUS PEASANTS

GERMANY. 1524–25

In the beginning, the peasants' rebellion met with stunning success. Under the banner of the Bundschuh, the individual bands which made up the peasants' army roamed the country almost unopposed, killing and looting, destroying and burning down castle after castle, cloister after cloister. Some towns were taken and some went over to the rebels' side.

By the beginning of 1525, almost all of Frankonia, Suevia, and some adjacent territories were in the rebels' hands. Yet just a few months later, the rebellion broke down completely, its failure the result of disunity, lack of competent leadership (in spite of the fact that some knights joined the cause and led the rebels), insufficient artillery, a scarcity of trained gunners, and the tendency of the peasants to run home at harvest time.

An estimated three hundred thousand peasants were slaughtered during the last battles, and the number who were cruelly executed afterward is beyond estimation. The spirit of rebellion among the German peasants was broken forever.

LANSQUENETS
GERMANY. CIRCA 1525

The medieval armies of the knights in armor were by now replaced by the lansquenets, or Landsknechte, mercenary soldiers who were mostly peasant lads or men of the lower urban classes.

These men were the first to express in their way of dress the spirit of the new times, with its craving for a freer, less repressed, and less hampered life. Whenever they felt hemmed in by a garment, they simply split it wide open in several places. At the same time, their urge to express the swagger and bravado which characterized the soldier's life led them to widen and multiply these slits and slashes beyond the demands of mere comfort. These they lined with other materials of flashy colors, intentionally disregarding any system or symmetry.

With every man suiting his own whim and taste, this style can hardly be considered the beginning of the military uniform. On the other hand, it had an enormous influence on civil costume throughout Europe.

REBELLIOUS PEASANTS

GERMANY. CIRCA 1525

Although the lansquenets in the last drawing were hardly dressed in what we would consider military attire, these fighters on the peasants' side have adopted two lansquenet articles that *are* somewhat soldierly. In particular, notice the broad sword and split hat worn by the man on the right. He, himself, may well have been a former lansquenet, since many of them, being of peasant stock, joined the rebellious bands. In fact, with their military discipline and training, they often formed the backbone of the rebels' fighting forces. There was even a point when the Emperor's own Landsknechte—who in the end brought about the defeat of the peasants—offered to go over to the side of the rebels. Foolishly, because they didn't want to share the booty, the peasants rejected them.

SOLDIERS' WIVES
GERMANY. CIRCA 1525

During the many wars of this era, culminating in the gigantic and devastating Thirty Years War in the seventeenth century, the armies were followed by long lines of carts carrying supplies and booty—but mostly women, the soldiers' wives and harlots.

It would be a mistake to assume that the women were there to attend only to the sexual needs of the men. The soldier had to have somebody who could take care of and carry his heavy arms and other equip-

ment, as well as the larger pieces of booty, and these tasks fell to his female companion. She also cooked and sewed for him and took care of him when he was sick or wounded.

It is not surprising that the fashion of puffs and slashes, which originated with the military and soon spread all over Europe, first found its way into the costume of the soldiers' women.

LANSQUENET AND CAMP FOLLOWER
GERMANY. CIRCA 1525

As indicated in this drawing, the relationship between the soldier and the camp follower was not always an untroubled one. The women endured sore hardships and ill-treatment and were, in addition, subject to what was often harsh military discipline maintained by the tough sergeant in charge of the baggage train.

The lot of the camp follower was dramatically portrayed a century later in *Die Landstörtzerin Courage*, a novel by Hans Grimmelshausen, whose most famous work, *The Adventurous Simplicissimus*, gives us a revealing and informative picture of the life of a soldier in the Thirty Years War.

PEASANTS

GERMANY. 1525–1550

Albrecht Dürer, one of the great artists of all time, took much of his inspiration from the everyday lives of ordinary people. Dürer and the other excellent engravers and woodcut-makers who followed him— Hans Schäufelein, Albrecht Altdorfer, Hans Baldung Grien, Hans Sebald Beham, and Urs Graf—all came from the people. They were true artisans, members of the guild of house painters, glaciers, and gilders. Dürer himself served his full time as an apprentice and underwent all the hardships of those years and the ones that followed as a traveling journeyman.

The new print-making techniques created an entirely new audience for works of art. People who could never have afforded the expensive miniatures commissioned by the rich and mighty were now able to enjoy representations of the lives of people like themselves, the peasants, cooks, demobilized soldiers, and other plain folk portrayed by Dürer and his followers.

PEASANTS
GERMANY. 1525–1550

The artist Hans Sebald Beham was a prolific recorder of peasants' life, especially when they were engaged in carousing, drinking, and making love. He, himself, was reputed to have devoted himself to these occupations all his life, and to have spent his last years keeping a disreputable tavern, which gave him ample opportunity to observe his subjects. His engravings are a source for this drawing.

Most of the peasants in this day and age wore swords or long knives, which they had to take off when they entered a town.

130

PEASANTS

GERMANY. 1525–1550

The wife in this drawing, also inspired by a Beham print, is taking her husband home from one of the parish fairs, which were celebrated by the immoderate drinking of beer and eating of enormous amounts of bacon or ham, with cabbage, bread, and cheese. Traditionally, the fairs ended in coarse, sometimes very lewd, dances to the sound of pipes, drums, horns, bagpipes, trumpets, fiddles, and lutes.

These rare celebrations should not give us a misleading picture of the daily life of the peasant, a life which was miserable and drab beyond description. He lived in a primitive house made of clay and wood, covered with straw. His daily food consisted of coarse black bread, millet pulp or boiled beans and lentils, and very little else. He drank water or whey. In years when the harvest was bad, the peasants hungered and died like flies.

MAN AND HORSEBOY

IRELAND. 1525–1550

Under his long, capelike cloak, the older man is wearing an even longer tunic, which was called a saffron shirt, or simply saffron, because it was usually dyed with saffron. It has the same wide sleeves that we can see on the boy's short saffron. Women also wore garments just like these. The horseboy in this drawing has on a pair of long, tight trousers held down by a band under his bare feet.

MAN AND WOMAN

IRELAND. 1525–1550

The young Irish lass in this drawing is a member of the middle class of townspeople. With the exception of her headpiece, worn over a pleated kerchief, her costume is no different from that of women of her standing all over western Europe.

The man is wearing the same kind of saffron we saw on the stable boy in the last drawing. Here, seen from the back, it is worn over another, longer tunic.

TOWNSPEOPLE

FRANCE AND SPAIN. 1525–1550

The Spanish visitor, who looks with admiration at the French girl passing by, is dressed in a simple tunic with the broad band of trimming that was typically Spanish.

By this time, lower-class women worked profession-ally in such crafts as sewing and embroidering lin-gerie, and making and decorating hats. The woman's dress is in the Gothic pattern, with the bodice and skirt cut in one piece with inserted godets. Her skirt is tucked up.

PEASANTS

SPAIN. 1525–1550

The life of the Spanish peasant, whether on the barren plains of Castile, the rocks of Aragon, or the olive groves of Andalusia, was an extremely hard and poor one. The authority of the lord was virtually unlimited; he had full jurisdiction over his tenants and they had to deliver over a considerable part of their produce to him. Even the very few peasants who owned the land they cultivated could barely extract enough out of it to feed themselves and their families. About two-thirds of the Spanish peasants at this time were destitute.

The peasants in this drawing are dressed for bad weather. The typically Spanish features of their dress are the woman's high wooden pattens, or clogs, and the man's stuffed breeches.

PEASANTS GOING TO MARKET

SPAIN. 1525–1550

Since there was no market for the peasants' products in their own villages, they took them to the
nearest town. The peasant who didn't own his own
land had to deliver the produce to the monastery or
the wealthy middle-class townsman who owned the
fields. Rarely could he keep more than half of the
harvest for himself, and out of this he still had to pay
the royal taxes. By the time the tax collector was

through, the peasant might be left with nothing but
an empty house. Many peasants deserted these
"homes," which were then sold to cover the taxes or
destroyed to sell the building materials.

The stiff Spanish hat, with its narrow brim and tall
conical crown, worn by the man on the left, was the
most popular hat for men of all classes throughout
Europe for a time.

MORISCOS

SPAIN. FIRST HALF OF SIXTEENTH CENTURY

Moriscos was the name the Spaniards gave to the conquered Arabs who chose baptism over expulsion. But like the baptized Jews (Maranos), the Moriscos were always suspected of returning to the beliefs and customs of their fathers, and were continually exposed to governmental persecution and mob violence.

The man in this drawing is a Morisco, although the only difference in his dress from that of any Spanish laborer is the way the leather soles are strapped to his ankles.

The woman's outfit, on the other hand, is entirely Moorish, with her green and white striped headdress over a red and white kerchief, short open white jacket, stuffed trousers, and footless stockings.

MORISCOS

SPAIN. FIRST HALF OF SIXTEENTH CENTURY

In less than a century, in 1610, all the remaining Moriscos would be expelled to Africa, and overnight Spain would lose more than a million of its most industrious inhabitants.

Meanwhile, the men in this drawing are probably Moriscos. The clothes on the man on the left are virtually pure Moorish—the intricate lacing of the thongs that hold his shoes soled to his feet; the cape with its long, false sleeves with the cutout for his arms, and the turban. Note particularly the hood beneath the turban with the long tab hanging down the back and inserted into the collar of his cape. In the original, taken from the Weiditz *Trachtenbuch*, the tab was depicted in the Moorish colors of blue, red, and white. The trousers on both men are also of Moorish origin.

SERVANTS

FRANCE. MID-SIXTEENTH CENTURY

The maid servant shows a piece of herb she has picked from the garden to an older woman, who could be either the housekeeper or the mistress of the house. The accomplishments of a Renaissance housewife were, of necessity, many and varied, since even a small household made its own beer, baked bread, and sewed most of its clothes. One of the housewife's tasks was to take good care of the servants, who were considered part of the household, and to punish them when they were negligent.

The slits and puffs in the older woman's dress show the German influence. The ring worn by the girl on her head is designed to carry heavier loads.

PEDDLER AND TOWNSMAN

GERMANY. MID-SIXTEENTH CENTURY

The broad sword carried by the peddler testifies to the danger of traveling in this day and age. In some parts of Germany, there was not only the probability of being attacked by robbers, but also the possibility of attack by wolves and bears.

Even so, the miserable conditions of the roads made it more expedient for people to travel by foot, if not on horseback, even when carrying heavy loads, rather than in one of the clumsy carts drawn by horses or mules. Although duties were levied by princes, towns, and other authorities for the upkeep of roads and bridges, hardly anything was ever done about them.

COOKS

GERMANY. MID-SIXTEENTH CENTURY

Compared to the Middle Ages, when emphasis in eating was on the quantity of food, not the quality, the art of cooking made progress during the Renaissance. Increased international commerce, especially traffic with the newly discovered territories, provided the cook with a greater variety of spices. These he used so generously that many of his dishes would have been disagreeable to our palates, and even contemporary critics deplored this excess seasoning. One wrote of "these criminal sauces and stews, poisoned with garlic and other spices, together with sweets and almonds, to ruin the palate of a Rhino . . ."

Fruits and vegetables were still harvested by some townspeople from gardens within the town, and were preserved by the housewife and her cook. Some households also raised and slaughtered chicken, swine, and cattle. They pickled and salted the meat and made their own sausages.

FISHMONGERS

ITALY. MID-SIXTEENTH CENTURY

Fish and seafood of all kinds were always an important item of the Italian cuisine, and one of the least expensive. Fish was also a welcome substitute for meat on the many meticulously kept fast days.

The fishmonger's shop was either connected to his house or set up on markets along the main roads and crossways. His day started early, usually with the cry of the rooster. He himself ate simply, sparsely, and irregularly. Breakfast might be a slice of bread washed down with a beaker of wine.

BUTCHERS
ITALY, MID-SIXTEENTH CENTURY

Despite the fact that meat did not play as important a part in the Italian diet as it did, for instance, in
Germany and France, the butchers' guild was a respected and politically influential one in most of the
towns. Lamb and pork appeared in greater quantities
in the markets than beef did, but even these meats were
usually reserved for special occasions.

PEASANTS

ITALY. MID-SIXTEENTH CENTURY

The husband and wife disputing the custody of the family savings are dressed in clothes that might have been worn by any western European peasant. So far, few regional peculiarities have developed in Italian peasant dress. In this drawing, only the man's hat and bag are typically Italian. His doublet with the short peplum, and the leggings held together in front by a codpiece could be seen all over Europe. The woman's whole outfit is international in style.

TAILOR AND CLOTH CUTTER
GERMANY. MID-SIXTEENTH CENTURY

From way back, tailors were the butt of crude jokes based on their alleged slightness of stature and timidity of nature. A popular song of this age went, "At their anniversary/ nine times ninety-nine tailors/ were dined a roast flea/ and wined one thimbleful."

In the cloth cutter's costume, we see the German style of the Renaissance, which stemmed from the soldiery, at its fullest development. The doublet has

been slit and slashed wherever possible. The breeches that went with these doublets were known as Pluderhosen. They were made of two pair of breeches, or bags. The narrower pair, of a heavy material slit into vertical strips, was worn over a very wide pair of thin material, which protruded freely through the strips. Sometimes, the outer pair of breeches was replaced by ribbons. The codpiece was replaced by a ribbon bow.

MILLER'S MEN

GERMANY. MID-SIXTEENTH CENTURY

For some reason, the miller's craft was not a very respectable one. The miller was not a free artisan, and on the social ladder he stood on the same rung as a city guard, collector of customs, or night watchman, only a step above the gravedigger, street sweeper, chimney sweep, barber, and the hangman. Even as late as the eighteenth century, the millers' and barbers' crafts were among the very few open to the sons of lower-class city servants.

The short trunks attached to stockings (trunk hose), worn by the man on the left, are all that remain of the flamboyant Pluderhosen we saw in the last drawing. The other man is wearing moderately stuffed trousers, tied above and below the knee and laced to the waist. At the back, the lacing has been loosened for comfort at work, revealing a pair of short breeches.

MINERS

AUSTRIA AND GERMANY. MID-SIXTEENTH CENTURY

Mining was a very old occupation in Germany, in some places dating back to the days of the Romans. Seignorial owners had their mines worked by serfs, who kept some of the proceeds against payment of a tribute. As early as the eleventh and twelfth centuries, miners were organized on a trade union basis.

The man on the left is an overseer in charge of work production. The other man is in charge of the wooden construction within the mines, which supported the adits and galleries.

The leather apron covering the back of the man on the left, like those worn by both men in the next drawing, is a characteristic garment of the miner. These aprons served as protection when the men slid down the mine shafts. The different staffs of the two men are marks of their office.

MINERS

AUSTRIA AND GERMANY, MID-SIXTEENTH CENTURY

Miners worked in narrow pits, usually in a stooping position. Ventilation was poor and there was little protection against seepage of water or gases.

At the time of the peasant rebellion of 1524, the miners of Tirol joined the rebels and demanded the expropriation of the mines, which the princes had pawned to big commercial houses. The movement failed at the same time as the rebellion did.

The man on the left is wearing a hooded jacket made of coarse linen or burlap. It was called Maximilian's mountaineer, after the Emperor, Maximilian I, who lived and hunted deer in the Tirol. Both men are wearing the leather-backed aprons we saw in the last drawing.

FISHERMAN AND HOUSEWIFE
GERMANY. MID-SIXTEENTH CENTURY

The housewife shows the fisherman the size fish she will need for her family's Friday night dinner. Dangling from one end of the rope hung over her belt is her pouch, usually made of brown leather and closed by a drawstring, which served the same purpose as a modern woman's handbag. From the other end hangs her key ring, to which she frequently added a little knife and such other housewifely tools as a pair of scissors, spoons, and a sewing kit.

Dressmaking techniques had advanced to the point where sleeves were set into the garment, although not, as in the modern manner, all around the armhole. Instead, they were fastened either at the back of the armhole or, as in this drawing, tied to the body of the garment by strings, allowing the shirt to protrude.

The fisherman wears a leather bib and breeches stuffed with animal hair, in the Spanish style, which has been adopted in Germany.

PEASANTS

ITALY. MID-SIXTEENTH CENTURY

Peasants were allowed to hunt, but only for small game like rabbits, porcupines, badgers, weasels, and little birds. This man, with his loose-bottomed short breeches, carrying his net and a big stick, is about to go a-hunting.

The girl uses her sickle to reap the grain in spots where the scythe won't reach. After being thrashed with a flail, the grain, along with flour and oil, were stored on the ground floor of the farmhouse, just as it is in Italy today.

FISH SALTERS

ANDALUSIA, SPAIN. 1550–1575

Along the coast of Spain, as in Italy, fishing and preserving fish played an important role in sustaining and occupying the population. Andalusia had been the heart of the Arab population in Spain. Its inhabitants were gay and vivacious, but also hot-tempered and quick to draw the knife. Their notorious love of color, however, is not reflected in the dull browns, blues, and ochres of the smocks and hose of these fish salters. The slashed rolls at their shoulders are typically Spanish, although by this time, like Spanish costume in general, the fashion had spread throughout Europe.

PEASANT WOMEN

FLANDERS. 1550–1600

The best source of information on the customs and costumes of the common man of this era is the work of Pieter Brueghel, the greatest of the many Netherlands artists who found inspiration in the lives of ordinary people. In his many paintings, some filled with innumerable figures, he made immortal the Flemish people of the sixteenth century.

Pieter Brueghel (also written Bruegel, Breughel, even Prigel) the Elder, was named after the village where he was born. With his art-dealer friend, Frankert, Brueghel visited village fairs and other drinking bouts, or introduced himself as a distant relative at weddings, where he took in every detail of the appearance of the guests.

The two women in this drawing are wearing typical Brueghel costumes.

PEASANTS

FLANDERS. 1550–1600

These Brueghel-inspired men are wearing coats in the two most important styles of the period. The man on the left (1) wears a wide peasant coat, open in front; the other (2) has on a short, tight doublet, laced in front. Although his doublet has no skirt, sometimes this coat did have a very short peplum.

Until now, leggings consisted of two separate pieces, pulled up and tied in place by a cord around the waist. At the beginning of this century, the two legs were connected—in back by an inserted godet, with the seat cut in a bowl-like curve (2a), and in front by a flap sewn to the leg pieces. The whole garment was kept up by a cord fastened under the coat or, as in our drawing, laced to the doublet.

PEASANTS AT WORK

FLANDERS. 1550–1600

The short breeches of Gallic origin were brought to Rome by the legionaries. Throughout the Middle Ages, they were worn by men all over Europe, mainly in cold weather under leggings. In fact, to wear them without coverings, except at work, was considered improper, especially in the towns. Even the guilds had rules against such immodest behavior as crossing the street with bare thighs. Men who went to mass without leggings might be fined heavily.

PEASANT WOMEN

LORRAINE. 1550–1600

Except for the headdress, a regional style of Lorraine, the costumes in this drawing are fairly representative of peasant dress throughout Europe in this era. As we can see, the waist has finally come into its own as the natural separation between clothing for the upper and the lower body. This made it possible to design a simple, circular skirt in a style accessible even to the poor.

The kerchief is the oldest type of protection for the female head. In bad weather, one could shape it into a hood by fastening the ends under the chin, or by wrapping a separate strip of material around the neck. This strip, when such stronger fastening was not required, could be folded and laid on top of the head-kerchief, as the two women in our drawing have done. Apparently it remained in place by virtue of its own weight, or perhaps it was fastened by an invisible pin.

WAGONER AND TRADER

BAVARIA. 1550–1600

Teams of four, eight, or even more, horses pulling heavy four-wheeled carts were driven by wagoners. It was a tough job and wagoners were a burly breed, notorious for their crude behavior and vile language.

Our wagoner, left, wears a special version of the peasant coat characteristic of his occupation. It has a short, smooth body with an attached pleated skirt. His very short breeches, held together in front by a big codpiece, are laced to the shirt, which he wears under his coat. Another set of laces holds his leggings to the bottom of the breeches, and over the leggings he has drawn up a pair of high, soft boots. A whistle hangs

from the cord around his neck, and attached to the bag showing beneath his coat is an inkhorn; he needed writing equipment for his lists of freight, receipts, bills, and so on.

In the original source for this costume, an illustration by Jost Amman, the colors reflect the flashy look that wagoners favored throughout history. The hat is green, the coat orange, the shirt blue, the leggings yellow, the breeches brown, and the codpiece yellow.

The trader's outfit is typical of that worn by lower-class townsmen. By now, a bow has been substituted for the codpiece.

BARBER AND PEASANT

GERMANY. 1550–1600

According to Hans Sachs, the shoemaker and poet, the barber (left) "prided himself not only for his skill in cutting hair and beard and in shaving, but also for his ability in preparing wholesome ointments, dressing and healing wounds, setting broken limbs, healing the French disease (syphilis), gangrene, and cataracts, and in performing bloodlettings whenever desirable," which in those days was done at the slightest prompting.

By now, as we can see in this drawing, a real distinction has developed between rural and urban costume. Peasants at work had no use for slits and slashes in their garments; even in their holiday dress they rarely and only tentatively adopted the new fashion. In town, however, it was taken up enthusiastically by people of all classes.

SHOEMAKERS

GERMANY. 1550–1600

To become a shoemaker, or almost any other kind of craftsman, one had to be a member of the guild. In Germany, a shoemaker's apprentice had to be born free and in wedlock, of German blood, and be without a criminal record. Naturally, he had to be a male. It was the duty of a master shoemaker to house and feed his apprentice, as well as to instruct him. The minimum apprenticeship was three years, but it often lasted considerably longer—Hans Sachs served six or eight years.

Once he graduated to the rank of journeyman, the shoemaker was expected to travel on foot, sometimes for as long as seven years, working for pay in different shops. Only then was he eligible to return to his town to become a master. To qualify, he had to be a citizen of the town and the head of his own household, and to pass the master's test, he had to deliver his "masterpiece." It is almost impossible to over-estimate the pride a sixteenth-century artisan took in his work. No master craftsman would have found satisfaction in turning out mass-produced parts instead of completely finished products.

In this drawing, the shoemaker on the left is working in his shirt sleeves. The other has on a simple doublet in the German style. Both men are wearing Pluderhosen.

CARPENTERS

GERMANY. 1550–1600

The woodworking crafts were divided into several guilds, among them carpenters, cabinetmakers, coopers, and carriage builders. Besides regulating the professional activities of their members, the guilds played an important part in shaping their social and private lives. Sick or impoverished members were supported out of the guild's treasury. On special days, such as that of the guild's patron saint or when the admission of new members was being celebrated, banquets with much eating, drinking, and singing were held. The composition, as well as the rendition, of the songs was taken very seriously and subject to strict rules, and a singing academy of master craftsmen met regularly.

In this drawing, the man on the right is wearing a costume of rural character; the other is dressed in more urban attire.

DISCHARGED SOLDIER AND PEASANT

GERMANY. 1550–1600

The vagrant soldier, still armed, cherishes the not entirely unjustifiable hope that he will be left alone by the count's forester, who certainly would have dealt harshly with any peasant caught poaching.

When soldiers were dismissed at the end of the campaign for which they had been hired, it was up to them to find a living for themselves. More often than not, the living took the form of highway robbery.

Many soldiers also deserted before they had served their time, even though to do so might mean severe punishment—in the conventional military phrase, "Nowhere should he find a safe hiding or peace."

The German military style, which, as we have seen, had spread throughout Europe, is now on its way out and is being replaced by Spanish-inspired fashions, as in the costume worn by the forester, right.

ENGLISH COMMONER AND GERMAN CHILD

GERMANY. 1550–1600

At this time, when love was not yet considered a necessary or even important prerequisite for marriage, the betrothal of small children was not restricted to the nobility, but extended to children of the higher middle classes and even some well-placed craftsmen. In Germany, the prosperity of Hamburg, Bremen, and other cities of the Hanse, as well as the commercial centers in the south, was such that even some small merchants were now rich enough to make their children desirable matches. The well-to-do English commoner in this drawing may well be eyeing the little German girl as a candidate for betrothal to his son.

Notice the lowered waistline of the man's doublet. This is more in the Spanish style than the German.

SAILORS

NORTHWEST GERMANY. 1550–1600

The boatswain, left, and the common sailor are both wearing typical sailors' trousers, with legs of equal width all the way down, and heavily lined. The origin of this fashion, which was not restricted to Germany, probably dates back to the short wide pants worn by men in Normandy as early as the tenth century.

The sailors' conical hats, usually red or brown in color, are also ancient in origin. Although they were made of heavy wool, they were worn indoors as well as out.

Sailors' clothes were usually dyed a brownish mixture of earth and tar. The pants were sometimes red or made of unbleached linen. In this drawing, only the boatswain's costume, with its ruff and small epaulets at the shoulders, shows any traces of the contemporary fashion in men's clothing.

162

FRISIAN SAILORS

GERMANY. 1550–1600

Frisians, who lived on the islands of the same name in the North Sea, were described as slender, with light-colored eyes and hair. They were said to be good-looking, but unpolished and rude. A contemporary treatise on manners warns, "Don't use your thumb for spreading butter as the Frisians do."

The long, wide sailors' pants which we saw in the last drawing were sometimes worn over another pair. In this case, the outer trousers, usually made of linen, were rolled up over a pair of long, woolen, inner pants. The hats on these men are a variation of the high, conical hats worn by the last pair of sailors.

FRISIAN WOMEN

GERMANY. 1550–1600

By the second half of this century, a variety of regional dress had evolved both in Germany and other countries of western Europe. In some places, even the towns and villages in one valley developed their own peculiarities of dress. Only a few examples of these regionalisms can be offered within the scope of this book.

The bells attached to the dresses worn by the women in this drawing had been used as ornaments in various parts of Europe in the fourteenth and fifteenth centuries. Because of the Frisian women's pre-

dilection for all kinds of metal decorations, however, they remained a part of the local fashion scene right through the sixteenth century, and even later. The favorite color of the Frisians was red, and all parts of the costumes on these two figures, except for the white headdresses, were red.

Like their men, the Frisian women were a rough lot. It was written of the women of Dittmarschen in the dukedom of Holstein that "They resemble fierce animals and wild she-wolves."

TWO WOMEN

SPAIN. 1550–1600

The characteristic dress of the peasant women of this time was totally unaffected by the fashion of upper-class women during the late Renaissance and the Baroque period. Most readers are familiar with that style, originating in Spain and adopted all over Europe—the tight bodice that completely flattened the bust and strangled the waist, the enormous sleeves, and the stiff skirt that made sitting down, and even walking, a problem.

A faint echo of that elegant, if unhealthy, fashion would be found in the dress of lower-class towns-women, like the figure at right, who often wore a great many petticoats—sometimes as many as twelve at a time!

PEASANTS

FRANCE. 1550–1600

These peasants might have lived anywhere in France during the time of the late Renaissance. Typical of all French peasant dress are the girl's short, tight bodice, laced in front, the pleated dress, the petticoat, and the small apron.

The man, too, is wearing the style of dress that was common in this period. His hat and trousers and the sleeveless smock with its rather long skirt are Spanish in origin.

MARKET PEOPLE

HOLLAND. 1550–1600

After liberation from the Spanish yoke, Holland's prosperity increased greatly. One manifestation of this influence was the quantity of alluring food in the markets. This display of colorful fish, lobsters, crabs, meat, fruits, and vegetables was a fine source of inspiration for the blossoming school of Dutch genre painters. Market people appeared in many of the works of the genre painters.

VINTAGERS

ITALY. 1550–1600

Although the Italian peasants' food was not scarce, it was of limited variety. The food for the whole day was cooked in the morning over a wood fire. A main dish of corn mash (polenta), chestnuts, and vegetables from their own gardens was prepared with olive oil. Sometimes this was supplemented with bread and a little pork or lamb. Wine was drunk regularly in Italy, even by the peasants.

The big vat filled with black grapes, from which the man is about to take a sample, will be pressed into the red wines of Tuscany.

PEASANT GIRL AND BASKET CARRIER

VENICE. 1550–1600

Basket bearers stationed themselves at the markets at the Rialto or San Marco to carry home the shoppers' merchandise. They had an excellent knowledge of the town—no mean achievement, as anyone who has ever had to find an address in Venice will understand.

At this time in Italy, as well as in France and Germany, the trend toward regionalisms in dress, especially in the country, was already well advanced. In Spain, it had started earlier. In England, regional differences in dress never were of any consequence.

The girl's outfit is basically Venetian, although the German military fashions have left their mark on the hat, shoes, and possibly the decorations on the dress that give the appearance of slashes.

PEASANT GIRL AND PROSTITUTE

ROME. 1550–1600

In Rome, prostitutes, right, had to identify themselves by wearing a yellow veil or wrapper. The number of prostitutes in the city was at times estimated at between six and eight thousand. In addition to the regular population, there were so many foreign travelers in Rome that it was considered necessary to tolerate the prostitutes in order to protect the safety of decent women, who were exposed to molestations in public even in daylight.

The peasant girl, who clearly has never before encountered a woman like this in her own village, is wearing a costume of specific Italian character, with far fewer regionalisms than the one worn by the girl in the last drawing.

170

JEW FROM PADOVA AND
WOMAN FROM GENOA

ITALY. 1550–1600

With their final expulsion from Spain in 1492, many Jews went to Italy, where they were confined to ghettos. Usually, although it is not shown in this drawing, a Jew had to identify himself by wearing a ring on a yellow cord around his neck. He also had to wear a broad, flat beret, either black, red, or yellow.

Otherwise the Jew's dress was no different from the dress of any other middle-class or lower-class man in towns all over Italy.

The woman is wearing a typically Genoan costume. Fastened beneath her shoes are pattens, known as zoccoli in Italian.

WOMAN FROM FLORENCE AND
VENETIAN BEGGAR

ITALY. 1550–1600

Unlike the regional costume worn by the woman from Genoa in the last drawing, this Florentine woman is dressed in an outfit that could be considered fairly representative of the costume of wives of small merchants and artisans in any Italian town. Beggars like the one approaching her for a handout were popularly known as the "bashful poor."

All over Europe throughout the Renaissance, municipal councils tried through their sumptuary laws to draw strict lines not only between clothes worn by the nobility and commoners, but also among the various classes of commoners. Servants were not supposed to dress like artisans, nor were artisans supposed to look like merchants or bankers. Even within this last group, there were special privileges for mayors, members of the city council, or members of patrician families. The laws were nowhere very successful.

PROSTITUTES

VENICE. 1550–1600

In Venice, the prostitutes lived mainly in the districts of San Samuele, San Apollinare, and San Geminiano. Residences along the Grand Canal were forbidden them, nor were they allowed to sleep in taverns. During Holy Week, they were not permitted to leave their quarters.

The women in this drawing are wearing cheap and gaudy imitations of upper-class costume. Under their skirts, many prostitutes liked to wear men's trousers, which they exposed at every opportunity, even in church where this outrage was frequently condemned from the pulpit. The extravagant hairdo of the woman on the left was also a definite mark of her trade.

173

GALLEY PRISONER AND MARINE

VENICE. 1550–1600

For crimes not punishable by death, a prisoner might be committed to a galley, sometimes for life. The prisoner's legs were chained to the bench on which he rowed, slept, lived, and often died. Occasionally, as here, he would be unchained in order to work on the land or to carry loads of wood, water, or other freight to and from the ship.

The prisoner's head and face were shaven, except for his moustache. His dress was a coarse cowl with a hood attached and a red sailor's hat. The marine in this drawing belongs to a kind of militia recruited from poor laborers, who were called up to man the galleys whenever needed. His cape also served him as a blanket.

PEASANTS
ENVIRONS OF VENICE. 1550–1600

Peasants from the countryside around Venice, from as far away as Treviso, brought cheese, fruit, vegetables, and chickens to the many markets of Venice. The biggest market of all was held every Saturday in San Marco.

Although serfdom in Italy was not as oppressive as in many other countries, and peasants were actually permitted to travel out of their districts or to enter the guilds in the towns, the peasant's life was still a very hard one. Nor did the Italians hold peasants in any higher regard than did the Germans or French. They are described in contemporary writings as "impolite," "malicious," "thieving," and "so dirty that they could be smelt from afar."

Peasant costume of the Renaissance is generally depicted in rusty browns and grays, faded blues and yellowish greens. Occasionally one part of the costume, for instance the hat or trousers, is shown in vivid hues.

GYPSY AND TUSCAN GIRL
ITALY. LATE SIXTEENTH CENTURY

Gypsies appeared in Central Europe about the beginning of the fifteenth century. Parts of the costume of the gypsy in this drawing—her headgear, ornaments, and the pattern of her dress—testify to the gypsies' Eastern origin, and have been retained unchanged to modern times.

Although sumptuary laws governing private luxury were still being promulgated, they were generally ignored. By her elegant appearance, it seems obvious that the young girl having her palm read has paid them little attention. Sumptuary laws decreed, among other things, the materials allowed for dresses, linings, and trimmings, the permissable length of trains, and the types of ornaments that might be worn. Peasants, for example, were strictly forbidden the wearing of silks, pearls, gold, and silver. In a typical sumptuary law, issued by Duke Johann Georg of Saxony in 1612, peasant men and women were permitted to wear clothing made only of leather, linen, and fustian; no velvet or satin, no embroidery, and no gold and silver. Similar restrictions were imposed on artisans and other townspeople of low rank, and on servants.

JESTERS
VENICE. END OF SIXTEENTH CENTURY

A favorite prank of the jesters at the Venetian carnival was slinging rotten eggs, particularly at the magnificent dresses of the ladies who appeared on the
balconies of the palaces.

This egg-slinger has disguised himself as a Spanish
nobleman, right. His ammunition-bearer—he might
have more than one—is wearing a fool's costume.

ARTISANS' WIVES

GERMANY AND NETHERLANDS. END OF SIXTEENTH CENTURY

The wrapper worn by these women dates back to the early Middle Ages and probably originated in Holland. It was worn from the lower Rhine valley eastward to Hamburg and Holstein, and also in Cologne, Frankfort, Nuremberg, and other towns to the south. Called the Hoike, or Huike, it was made from heavy, dark material and pressed into folds. At the neck, a small collar of varying length and width was inserted, which in good weather stood up behind the head, and in bad weather could be pulled forward to form a "roof" over the face.

The small, goffered edging at the neck of the blouse developed into the large fluted cartwheel toward the end of the century. Although it was worn by men and women of all ranks, it was never worn in its most exaggerated dimensions by members of the lower classes.

FRISIAN PEASANT AND HUNTER
GERMANY. END OF SIXTEENTH CENTURY

The first known attempt to document a European native costume was made by a sixteenth-century Frisian chief, Unico Manninga, who kept a chronicle in which he included colored illustrations of the Frisian dress worn by his ancestors, as far back as 1500.

The regional flavor of Frisian costume was to be found primarily in the styles worn by the island women. (See the drawing on page 164.) The clothes worn by the Frisian men differed hardly at all from the common man's dress all over Germany. In fact, the wide trousers on our peasant, left, were worn pretty much throughout Europe by sailors and other men living close to the sea. The hat on both of the men in this drawing was very popular all over Germany with peasants, hunters, and wagoners. Its brim was cut in such a way as to make it possible to turn down the back and sides. Actually, it is very similar to hats worn by winter sportsmen in America today.

POMERANIAN PEASANTS
GERMANY. END OF SIXTEENTH CENTURY

Custom demanded that a girl appear indifferent toward an admirer's approaches. Even if a boy was a serious suitor, and an acceptable one, she had to reject his proposal three or four times before she accepted it.

Both of these peasants are wearing clothes of very simple design; except for the girl's conical hat, they can hardly be considered regional. The young lady's Brüstling, a short, sleeveless bodice worn over a regu-lar bodice, was popular in town and country throughout Germany. The man's trousers, of ancient design, are of a type already discovered among the pre-Roman findings in the marshlands of Thorsberg and Dannersdorf. They later became popular with the sansculottes of the French Revolution, and are, in fact, the forerunner of the kind of pants men wear today.

SAXON PEASANTS

GERMANY. END OF SIXTEENTH CENTURY

The shoulder covering of the woman is the same kind of Brüstling we saw on the girl in the last drawing. Here, in the rear view, it displays rudiments of a Spanish collar. The skirt, which is tucked up, and the apron are also similar to those worn by the Pomeranian peasant girl.

The man is dressed in an outfit that was made popular by the mercenary soldiers during the first part of the century.

FOREIGN MUSICIAN AND JUGGLER

ENGLAND. END OF SIXTEENTH CENTURY

Spanish and French musicians, jugglers, and acrobats performed in the streets of London and other European cities. The acrobats had a repertoire of jumps and capers, known under such names as "the monkey's leap," "the hare's leap," "the cat's leap," "the trout's leap," and so on.

The musician's stiff, high hat, his wing collar, and trunk hose all testify to the fact that by this time Spanish fashions were dominant throughout Europe.

The source for these costumes is a sheet of the Roxburghe Ballads. Printed sheets of ballads had been popular in England as far back as the fifteenth century. They sold by the thousands in town and country in Shakespeare's day, and continued to be published throughout the eighteenth century. In a way, they were comparable to the illustrated magazines of our own day, and were part of the collections of the early fifteenth-century libraries.

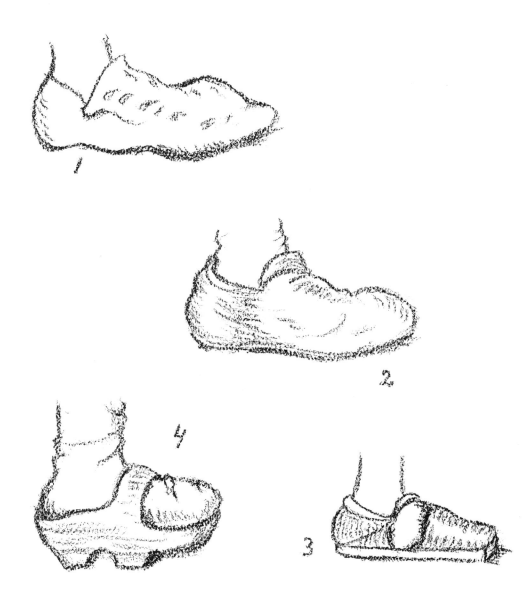

SHOES WORN BY THE LOWER CLASSES

LATE SIXTEENTH CENTURY

1. Artisan's shoe, black or colored leather. Second half of sixteenth century.

2. Peasant's shoe, black leather. Second half of sixteenth century.

3. Housewife's shoe, black leather with wooden sole. End of century.

4. Woman's leather stocking on leather patten. End of century.

PEASANT HATS
NETHERLANDS. SIXTEENTH AND SEVENTEENTH CENTURIES

These are among the many styles of hats worn by the peasants in the paintings of Ostades, Teniers, Brouwers, and the Brueghels:

Felt hats with crowns of varying heights and shapes and brims of different widths (1, 4, and 6);

Felt hats with no brim at all (3); and

Fur hats with the brim rolled up (2).

Coifs (5) were worn under the hat, or with no hat at all.

The beret (7), which in town was the most favored headgear of the Renaissance, was also popular with peasants in France, the Netherlands, and Italy. It was rarely worn by peasants in Germany.

Seventeenth Century

WAGONERS

ITALY. EARLY SEVENTEENTH CENTURY

In the Middle Ages, artists depicted their biblical subjects in the costume of their own age, thus making those paintings a reliable source of information about the appearance of the common people of that era. Even before the seventeenth century, however, some knowledge was available about ancient dress, and Renaissance artists had already begun to apply this knowledge to their work. For this reason the larger number of Renaissance and Baroque paintings of biblical and antique subjects can no longer be considered a reliable source for the costumes of the common man of their day.

Luckily for us, however, there were graphic products, as those by Annibale Carracci, which did take their inspiration from everyday life. Carracci published a series of prints of the different types of people he saw on the streets of Italian towns. The wagoners in this drawing were taken from that series.

KNITTER AND CLIENT
ITALY. EARLY SEVENTEENTH CENTURY

Among Carracci's Italian street types was the ambulant knitter (1) seen here with an apparently dissatisfied client.

The art of knitting dates back to the sixteenth century, and by now knitted stockings—silk for nobles, wool for everyone else—had pretty much supplanted the sewn style. Peasants, however, still preferred the older kind, which were sewn together from pieces of leather, cloth, or linen, and then cut to fit. Actually, even in the knitted stockings gores were inserted to provide width. The gores also offered an opportunity for colorful decorations, as we can see from the stocking in the knitter's hand.

Both men in this drawing are wearing short, heavily padded breeches. The man on the left wears his over another, longer pair. Note, too, the different ways their sleeves are attached to their smocks. For greater freedom of movement, the knitter's sleeves are fastened to the smock at one edge only. The sleeves worn by his client are set into his smock with a deep corner at the back.

MAID AND COOK
VENICE. EARLY SEVENTEENTH CENTURY

These two domestic servants are probably on their way to church. The modest maid hides within her big, scalloped shawl, but the cook obviously sees no reason to conceal either her charms or her elegant outfit, including her baroque fan.

Good cooks were extremely important people and very well paid. Kitchens in the wealthy homes in Venice were so ostentatious that the magistrate some-

times fined a household for such excesses as using too costly materials for kitchen utensils, for having too big, or too many, stoves, and for overdoing the decorations of their tables.

In addition to their culinary ability, cooks were supposed to be healthy, polite, and not given to drinking.

FISHERMEN

VENICE. EARLY SEVENTEENTH CENTURY

In Venice, the fishing business was plagued by inter-mediaries, and ordinances were repeatedly passed to control the activities of jobbers, who made huge fortunes forcing up the market price of fish, while keeping the profit to the poor fisherman low.

Professional fishermen, such as these two taken from an engraving by Giuseppe Mittelli, used nets much like those still used in Italy today.

The sash on the man to the left is the one characteristically worn by Italian laborers. The shirt on his companion, with its wide sleeves and small cuffs, is of a type worn all over Europe.

REBELLIOUS PEASANTS
BOHEMIA. EARLY SEVENTEENTH CENTURY

Unrest among the peasants was nothing new in Bohemia. It had reached its peak in the fifteenth century, with the uprisings of the followers of the reformer John Huss. After initial success, that rebellion was bloodily suppressed, but it was never forgotten by the Czech people. Among their cherished legends is one about the cave of Blanik, where the slain heroes wait for the hour of a new liberation of Bohemia. Minor peasant uprisings continued into the eighteenth century.

The imprint of Spanish fashion has extended even to these peasants who lived far to the east of Spain. Note particularly the stuffed rolls around their shoulders.

CELLARMEN

GERMANY. EARLY SEVENTEENTH CENTURY

The turn of the century brought little change in costume generally, and even less in the costume of the common man.

The costume source for this drawing of two workers in a wine cellar is a leaflet showing a view of Heidelberg in 1608. Small figures were frequently used to decorate maps and "views" and these are an excellent source of information on the life of the people.

HESSIAN PEASANTS
GERMANY. EARLY SEVENTEENTH CENTURY

Early in the seventeenth century, sashes, like the one worn by the man on the right, began to replace the belt.

The other peasant is dressed in rather old-fashioned clothes—a long variation of the peasant coat and leggings, also in the old style, held together in front by a triangular flap with an inserted codpiece. Of particular interest is his big hat in a style that had long been favored by peasants. During the Thirty Years War (1618–1648) it found its way into the armies, when many peasant boys either volunteered. or were conscripted. Since there were no regular uniforms for them, they wore their own clothes, including their hats. Other soldiers discovered that the peasant hat was more comfortable than the stiff Spanish hat, and adopted it. Eventually the style spread to the officers and to civilians, too.

TOWNSPEOPLE

GERMANY. EARLY SEVENTEENTH CENTURY

In olden days, rain turned the roads into seas of mud, passable only by means of planks or paving stones, or, in extreme cases, by walking on stilts. But town maintenance began to improve during the Renaissance, and by now the streets were tolerably clean and partially paved.

The costume source for the clothes worn by this couple was the previously mentioned Heidelberg leaflet, published in 1608.

PEASANTS FROM MECKLENBURG
GERMANY. EARLY SEVENTEENTH CENTURY

Except for the contemporary Spanish ruff at their necks, both of these country people are wearing traditional old German peasant costume. The woman has donned a little sleeved jacket over her bodice. An apron completely covers her skirt; a pair of mittens are tucked into the band. The man wears a peasant coat of the simplest cut over a smock, and the very old style of trousers.

GUEST AND SERVANT IN AN INN

SPAIN. EARLY SEVENTEENTH CENTURY

Our guest is so anxious to leave the inn, where he has spent a restless night fighting off fleas and other vermin, that he hasn't even taken the time to button his gaiters. According to contemporary sources, conditions in Spanish inns during the seventeenth century were no better than they were in the Middle Ages.

The appearance of the slatternly servant seems to bear out those reports.

Few Spaniards turned to the despised occupation of innkeeper, leaving the job to foreigners, mostly Italians.

196

ROBBERS

PARIS. EARLY SEVENTEENTH CENTURY

About a sixth of the population of Paris was virtually destitute. People slept under bridges, in barges on
the river, and in any corner where they might find
some protection from the elements. Beggars poured
into the city from the countryside, where conditions
were even worse. Many of them became petty thieves

—in Les Halles, vendors and buyers were fleeced in
broad daylight-—while others took to highway robbery.
The number of robbers was also increased by demobilized or deserting soldiers, like the man on the right
in this drawing.

JESTERS
PARIS. EARLY SEVENTEENTH CENTURY

On any day of the year, professional fools and jesters played their pranks on the Pont Neuf, the old meeting place for all kinds of performers and charlatans. But on special days devoted to pleasure, such as New Year's Eve or the feasts of St. Jude or St. Simon, other young men disguised themselves as fools and beat passersby and each other with swine bladders or bunches of straw attached to sticks.

VINTAGERS

FRANCE. EARLY SEVENTEENTH CENTURY

The merry mood of this couple, who have celebrated the harvest with a generous intake of the new wine, should not make us forget that French vintagers, most of them day laborers, were no better off than any French peasants.

The reforms of King Henry IV, one of the very rare rulers to care about the people, did not outlast him, and after his death the already low wages of the vintagers were cut in half. When they returned from their work in the evening, these laborers could look forward to a meal of cabbage soup and bread, with an occasional piece of cheese for a special treat. The working day was from sunrise to sunset.

The shirt worn by the man in this drawing was cut diagonally into two lobes, which were then crossed over the chest. Here, one of the pieces has been left unfastened to show the construction.

TRAVELER AND HIGHWAYMAN
ENGLAND. EARLY SEVENTEENTH CENTURY

Even in daylight, every main road in England was plagued by highwaymen, just as in the old days. Moreover, as they were mounted on fine horses, the highwaymen could easily outride the inadequate (and often reluctant) security forces that patrolled the roads.

Some of the robbers were scions of respectable, even noble, families, and the costume of the robber in this drawing suggests that he might be one of these, with his fine ruff, lace cuffs, and elegant shoes. The robbers were surrounded by a certain glamour, which

did not, however, prevent their admirers from enjoying the spectacle of their hangings, since hangings were about the most popular entertainment of this period.

The traveler, who may well be shaking in his shoes, is dressed in the clothes of a small-town Englishman. His Spanish doublet has a deep waistline and his Spanish-style breeches, less padded than they were in the sixteenth century, resemble two hanging bags, fastened by string below the knees.

"WILD IRISH" COUNTRY FOLK
IRELAND. EARLY SEVENTEENTH CENTURY

Not much has changed in the costume of the Irish since Albrecht Dürer drew it at the beginning of the sixteenth century. The saffron shirt and the blanket, which also served as a cloak, were two of the most important elements. In this drawing, the woman's blanket is lined with fur; the man's is patterned wool with a fringe. Since the weather is cold, the man has pulled soft leather stockings over his tight leggings. The woman's legs are protected by a wrapping of broad strips of some coarse material.

This costume was taken from the figures decorating Speed's map of Ireland, published in 1610. At about this time English costume was enforced in Ireland and Irish dress began to decline.

COMMONER AND BOY

ENGLAND. 1600–1650

Ballads printed as leaflets sometimes included illustrations showing the everyday dress of the lower classes. These ballads played an important part in their lives, giving voice to their grievances, aversions, and affections, and serving as their newspapers.

The doublets and the padded trousers indicate that the Spanish influence was still very strong in England.

GYPSIES

FRANCE. 1600–1650

The woman on the left is wearing a collection of derelict, nondescript articles of clothing; her hat must have belonged to a soldier. Parts of the costume on her companion point to the Eastern origin of the gypsy tribe. The very long skirts on both are typical of gypsy costume right up until modern times.

The outfit on the little boy, on the other hand, was either handed down by a wealthy family or stolen. It could be that the boy, himself, was stolen, since gypsies were always accused of stealing children. Even as late as the eighteenth century, we find ordinances forbidding children to leave the immediate surroundings of their villages for fear that they will be abducted by the gypsies.

GYPSIES
FRANCE. 1600–1650

Jacques Callot, whose engravings of traveling gypsies were the costume source for this drawing and the last, was probably the greatest delineator of beggars, vagabonds, wandering gypsies and actors, and other ragged types. Callot was born in Nancy in 1592. As a very young apprentice in a glass-painting studio, he ran away with the wandering gypsies. Fortunately for posterity, he was eventually found and forced back to the workshop.

The outfit of the man at left stems mainly from the soldiery; the clothing of the other gypsy shows strong oriental traits.

WATER VENDOR AND CUSTOMER
ROME. 1600–1650

The days when Rome could boast of eleven work-ing aquaducts and a plentiful supply or pure water were long since past, and polluted water was the cause of much illness and infection. Save for the Aqua Virgo, which flowed intermittently into the fountain of Trevi, and a few other sources, water could only be obtained from the Tiber and the wells. This made the trade of the aquariciarii, who brought pure water to the city in barrels strapped to the backs of donkeys, and sold it on the streets, a quite lucrative one.

The fringed sash worn by the man on the right, and the high hat on the other man are styles frequently shown in Rome during the first half of the seven-teenth century. Both the doublets and the breeches are thickly padded.

MASKED REVELERS

VENICE. 1600–1650

The freedom offered by the opportunity to wear masks was welcome indeed to citizens held under tight rein by their Republic. For months afterward, people used the excuse of the annual carnival to continue wearing their masks—sometimes for as long as half a year.

"The mask is the most convenient thing in all the world," wrote playwright Carlo Goldoni. "It facilitates all intrigues and daring enterprises." Masks served lovers as well as criminals, political plotters, and other opponents of the government.

The "woman" behind the female mask on the right is actually a man.

TOWN MOB LOOTING A GHETTO

GERMANY. 1600–1650

Jews first settled in Frankfurt in the sixteenth century and, as everywhere, they were confined to a ghetto. The fact that Jews were in general protected by the princes and other authorities, for whom they supplied money and goods, did not prevent occasional outbreaks of mob violence.

The man on the left is an artisan who has apparently come directly from his shop, since he is wearing his working smock. The hammer in his belt will be used to smash windows and doors in the Jewish quarter. The other man's hat, two doublets, and padded trousers show the Spanish influence still dominating lower-class male costume.

DISCHARGED SOLDIERS

GERMANY. 1625–1650

The strong influence of the lansquenets, or Landsknechte, on sixteenth-century fashion was nothing compared to the impact that the costume of soldiers in the Thirty Years War had on male and female European fashion in the seventeenth century.

To mention just a few of the most important garments that can be directly traced to that war:

The soldier's soft hat, with its broad brim and low crown, fathered the tricorn. His trapezoidal leather jerkin became the justaucorps. His soft, broad collar became the extremely popular "falling band," a flat collar that ended in two points.

Men of all ranks and occupations, including small merchants and artisans, imitated the soldier by carrying swords and wearing spurred boots, even if they never went near a horse. The rows of buttons decorating the seams of the soldier's trousers, supposedly used as a reserve of lead for casting bullets, also became part of the civilian fashion scene.

SERVANT AND TOWNSMAN

HOLSTEIN, 1625–1650

German towns had grown and by the beginning of the century were enjoying a certain degree of prosperity. With the Thirty Years War, and the burning and plundering of the armies, this momentum came to an end. After the war, life in the cities, although not completely extinguished as in some rural areas, was arid and barren.

The simple costume worn by the servant woman displays no national origin and might have been seen on anyone of her class in any part of Europe. The man's outfit still shows the dominant Spanish influence.

JEWS

GERMANY. 1625–1650

The man wears on the sleeve of his coat and on his cloak the yellow ring that Jews had been ordered to display on visible sections of their garments in 1452. Instead of the pointed yellow hat, which had been compulsory in the Middle Ages, in most towns Jews were now required to wear a big flat beret, either red, black, or yellow. The man's coat also indicates that he is a Jew; it is the old caftan, of oriental origin, brought by the Jews to Germany in the early Middle Ages. This is a shortened version and is open and buttoned in front.

Women had to border their dresses with blue stripes, but otherwise their costume did not differ from that of the gentile.

MASON AND MASTER BUILDER
GERMANY. 1625–1650

During and after the Thirty Years War when whole cities, such as Magdeburg, were completely destroyed, there was much work for construction workers, rebuilding fortifications and the damaged parts of the towns.

The man on the right wears a sleeveless short shirt over a doublet with slashed sleeves. A soft piece of leather tied around his waist serves as an apron.

PEASANTS

FRANCE. 1625–1650

Although rural life was far from the romantic idyll
portrayed in some of the literature of the seventeenth
and eighteenth centuries, it was not completely devoid
of pleasure and gaiety either. Festivals were celebrated
by the whole village on the patron saint's day and
other religious occasions, as well as at the end of the
harvest, especially if it was a good one.

WOMAN AND COBBLER

FRANCE. 1625–1650

The cobbler eying the somewhat hopeless job he is being handed wears a piece of animal skin, with the horn still attached, on top of his beret as a mark of his profession. His slightly padded breeches are in the ubiquitous Spanish style.

The majority of artisans—although by no means all, or in all places—were organized into corporations, sometimes called metiers or corps de metiers, which were the equivalent of the guilds. The master craftsmen were at permanent odds with the journeymen, or campagnons, primarily over the questions of food and wages. So many masters were less than honest in their dealings that at the end of the sixteenth century they were ordered to redeem in money the meals usually taken by journeymen at the masters' board.

BEGGING PILGRIMS
FRANCE. 1625–1650

Beggars roamed the roads among the bands of pilgrims on their way to St. Jacques de Compostelle and other famous places of worship. Because of the consideration generally shown to pilgrims, beggars often adopted the pilgrim staff and attached a shell, or coquille, the emblem of St. Jacques, to their hats and other parts of their clothing. Besides collecting alms, they sold such "real" relics as feathers from St. Michael's wings or straw from the manger, and, in passing, stole chickens and grapes.

Actually, many sincere pilgrims, who had started out with insufficient funds or had been cheated or robbed of their money, resorted to begging to get to their destination.

(As a culinary aside, it is interesting to learn the origin of the name of Coquilles St. Jacques—scallops gratinéed in their shells.)

PEASANTS

FRANCE. 1625–1650

Even well into the seventeenth century, writers were still describing French peasants as "looking like wild animals, burned by the sun yellow and black, obstinately digging in the ground from dawn to dusk, retiring to their caves at night, living on black bread and water." Exaggerated as this description sounds, it is borne out by many similar testimonies.

But in some regions, such as the Languedoc, and in the neighborhoods of the bigger towns, as well as during limited periods of peace and prosperity, the condition of the peasants was better.

MULETEER AND WOMAN TRAVELER
SPAIN. 1625–1650

In Spain, even more than in other countries, the mule was the principal means of transportation for people and goods. A journey on a mule saddle between two loaded baskets was cheap, but almost unbearably cold and uncomfortable in bad weather. It was also slow, but no slower than the journey on a mule-drawn, heavy wooden wagon on the abominable roads.

In the mountain regions, muleteers drove long trains of loaded pack mules along perilously steep and narrow tracks. In their perpetual struggle with the most stubborn and treacherous animal in the world, the mule drivers developed manners and language rude enough to surpass even those of the wagoners of other countries.

POOR TRAVELERS

ENGLAND. 1625–1650

These people are facing the strains of a long voyage, which were not negligible in those days. Everybody, including those traveling by private coach, had to endure the hardships caused by the deep, pitted highways. In the dark, the road was often indistinguishable from the surrounding heath and there was always the danger of being set upon by the numerous highwaymen.

While there were not yet stage coaches for people, there was a kind of stage wagon for goods, into which a few miserable souls could be cramped together in the straw. Poor people who were not prevented by infirmity or the weight of their baggage, preferred to travel on foot.

The Spanish influence on the costume of the common people lasted longer in England than in most other European countries. We see here an example of it in the woman's bodice and in the man's doublet and heavily padded breeches. The collars and hats reflect the Dutch influence.

PEASANTS FROM BASEL

SWITZERLAND. MID-SEVENTEENTH CENTURY

In most of Switzerland, serfdom had been abolished and although there were occasional uprisings, peasants were generally better off than they were in any other European country. This greater prosperity found its expression in the costume of the peasants. The man in this drawing might be mistaken for a rich burgher or even a member of the nobility. Actually, if we look closely, we can see that his impressive coat is really nothing but the old peasant coat with fashionably puffed sleeves and a pleated skirt.

But common men were not supposed to look like nobles, and this trend in dress gave rise to a new code of sumptuary laws forbidding the use of velvet, satin, silk, and other costly materials for the lower classes.

The regional characteristics to be seen in the woman's dress are in her hat and bodice.

218

PEASANT GIRLS FROM BASEL
SWITZERLAND. MID-SEVENTEENTH CENTURY

In the villages, unmarried girls gathered together during the long winter evenings to sing, knit, and weave. They were joined by the boys for dances and games, a custom frowned upon by the authorities. Other forbidden pleasures included christening feasts and even the giving of baptismal gifts exceeding a certain value: not more than half a crown or some cheese.

The girl on the right wears a hat in the style that was popular throughout the Upper Rhine valley, from Strassbourg to Basel, among men as well as women. Women wrapped their braids around the crown, as our girl has, or else let them hang down.

TOWNSWOMEN

ENGLAND. MID-SEVENTEENTH CENTURY

Around the middle of the seventeenth century, the leading influence on European costume passed from Spain to France. In England, French fashions were favored by the nobility, but among the lower classes, it was the Dutch and Puritan influence that prevailed. This simple, restrained clothing was made of coarse gray or black wool, cut in old-fashioned lines.

The long, white linen aprons were sometimes bordered with lace, but not if the wearer was actually one of the Puritans, who also eschewed the use of lace on their collars, cuffs, and caps.

The child is dressed exactly like an adult, as was the custom everywhere. Just as discipline in workshops and schools was strict, so it was in the family, where servants and children were frequently beaten.

INNKEEPER AND COOK
ENGLAND. MID-SEVENTEENTH CENTURY

For a long time, English inns had been enjoying a much better reputation than those on the continent. They were generally clean and the food and wine were tolerable. The innkeepers were no longer described as tyrants, but as the servants of their guests. Still, wagoners and other humble guests did not always have reason to be quite so happy about their lodgings and food. And some landlords and their servants were still suspected of furnishing the highwaymen with as much information about valuables and itineraries as they could worm out of the travelers.

In contrast to the costume we saw on the townswomen in the last drawing, these men are dressed in clothes that retain the Spanish influence.

SAILOR AND MAID

ENGLAND. MID-SEVENTEENTH CENTURY

The bodice and skirt of the maid's outfit are in a rusty red color, the petticoat is orange, and the collar and apron are white. Her black hat with the high crown and soft brim, undecorated except for a simple cord, is typically English for this period and not exclusively Puritan. Housewives and maids put these hats over the white caps which they always wore.

In addition to cleaning and cooking, housework included many other tasks, such as spinning and weaving, sewing, and preserving fruits, meat, and vegetables.

CATCHPOLE AND BEGGAR

ENGLAND. MID-SEVENTEENTH CENTURY

Lower-class lawbreakers could not expect much mercy, either from the authorities or from the crowds, who enjoyed the spectacle of their punishment. If a criminal was sentenced to be tied to the cart's tail-piece and whipped through the town, the spectators eagerly demanded that the whipping be administered with a will.

English beggars were just as noisy and impudent as those on the continent. They surrounded elegant coaches whenever they got the opportunity and harassed the occupants. Sometimes the attacks ended in murder.

SAILORS

HOLLAND. MID-SEVENTEENTH CENTURY

With the decline of the Spanish Netherlands and the merchant cities of Italy, competition for control of the maritime trade was between the English and the Dutch. Life and discipline on Dutch vessels were as hard and strict as on those of any other nationality.

The trousers on the sailor to the left are of the same ancient style as those worn in Frisia, Mecklen-burg, Pomerania, and other seashore communities. They were held around the body by means of a draw-string and the two legs were connected in front by the insertion of a gore. The other sailor's heavily padded breeches, of an entirely different design, are also typical sailor pants. They show the Spanish influ-ence, which was still very strong in Dutch costume.

CRIPPLE AND PEASANT BOY
HOLLAND, MID-SEVENTEENTH CENTURY

In Holland, where peasants fought at the side of noblemen and burghers for the freedom of their country, many painters, tired of the repetitive religious and mythological themes inherited from the Renaissance, found the peasants' daily life a worthy subject for art. In these paintings, therefore, we find an abundant source for every kind of Dutch peasant dress, including these examples from the work of Adrian van Ostade.

As in the Middle Ages, cripples and other deformed people were still considered amusing rather than deserving of pity. Dwarfs were the favorite entertainers in many a prince's court.

BARKER AT A FAIR AND CHILDREN
HOLLAND. MID-SEVENTEENTH CENTURY

The barker is displaying his tricks in front of a show tent to attract customers. He has tried to give a fancy note to his peasant clothes by adding a pleated collar and cuffs, a wooden sword, and a high, pointed hat, the mark of the buffoon.

The children, especially the little girl with her big straw hat on top of a cap, her laced bodice, and long, tucked-up skirt, are dressed exactly like little adults.

PEASANTS

HOLLAND. MID-SEVENTEENTH CENTURY

Skittle alleys became popular at the beginning of the century, and by now peasants at a game of skittles was a favorite subject for Dutch genre painters. Artists no longer were supported primarily by commissions, but produced pictures to be sold on the open market, much as most painters do today. Their products were often offered in stalls at a fair or on the street, and with competition as keen as it was, the safest way to achieve material success was to specialize in a certain subject. Many of the minor masters reproduced the same scene again and again with only slight variations.

DESERTING SOLDIERS

SPAIN. MID-SEVENTEENTH CENTURY

Both of these men are battered and worn, reduced
to living on what they can find or steal. In Spain
many men entered the armed forces out of a spirit of
adventure or in the hope of obtaining loot. Disen-
chanted, some deserted at the first opportunity and
came home as rowdy spongers or beggars or even robbers, with no funds and unfit for any legitimate work.

The man on the right is dressed strictly according
to Spanish fashion in a doublet with padded belly,
and tightly padded breeches ending in frilled cuffs,
one of which is torn off. His companion has adopted
the Swedish-German soldier's jerkin. Both wear the
typical high, stiff Spanish hat.

PEASANTS

SPAIN. MID-SEVENTEENTH CENTURY

Except when they dressed up in their regional costumes, Spanish peasants dressed so poorly, in torn and
tattered clothes, as to be an object of derision to
townspeople. Only on the man on the left can we
discern any characteristic national costume: the pic-
turesque draping of his blankets, and the canvas or
leather shoes in a cut worn generally by the peasants
of Spain.

Diego Velasquez (1599–1660) is best known for his
paintings of royalty. He was also keenly interested in
the appearance of peasants and laborers, however,
and some of his paintings show the kind of costume
drawn here.

PEASANT WOMEN
FRANCE. MID-SEVENTEENTH CENTURY

The clothes worn by peasants at work differed very little from one country to another. Regional characteristics in dress are to be found mostly in their Sunday-best costumes.

The costume source for this group of drawings of French peasants are some of the paintings by Louis Le Nain (1593–1648), one of the few French painters of this period to choose the daily life of peasants for his subject. In his paintings he captured the grave, reticent, resigned attitude of the peasants toward their hard life. The rusty browns and other dull hues are characteristic colors he used for his peasants' clothes.

230

PEASANTS AT A WEDDING

FRANCE. MID-SEVENTEENTH CENTURY

These jesters are really peasants dressed in the fancy costumes they wore on festive occasions, like weddings, which were celebrated with a great deal of eating and drinking. Sometimes the festivities went on for days. Ribald songs were sung and practical jokes played—and one can be sure that our two jesters took a leading part in playing them. After the newly-weds retired, they would be disturbed in a variety of ways; attempts to break into their bedchamber were among the more refined.

After the wedding was over, intoxicated guests used to proceed into the village or the next town. They turned over the stalls and booths, tossed wagons into the river, and in general behaved like drunken revelers of any age.

PEASANTS' DANCE

FRANCE. MID-SEVENTEENTH CENTURY

There were more frequent celebrations during times of peace in the second half of the century. In the good season an estrade was built on the village green for the band and a table was set with such delicacies as rabbit pie, roast pork and lamb, and wine; one ate, drank, and danced immoderately. But the long wars of Louis XIV, starting in the last quarter of the century, soon put an end to these good times.

The man wears a type of peasant coat which we have seen often in Germany. Caps like the one the girl is wearing have become the most popular female headcovering.

PHYSICIANS

FRANCE. MID-SEVENTEENTH CENTURY

Although surgeons and doctors with a university degree enjoyed considerable respect, your average physician was considered an artisan about on the level of barber—in fact, the two crafts were frequently combined. Nevertheless, artisans of even these lowly crafts adopted the costume of the upper classes, to a degree, and liked to dress à la mode.

The prints of Abraham Bosse (1602–1676), the most outstanding of a group of engravers who represented the lives of lower-class people, are a good source for this kind of costume.

PEASANTS

ITALY. MID-SEVENTEENTH CENTURY

This man and woman are dressed in their everyday working clothes, which are similar to those of virtually any European peasant of the era.

A contemporary writer accused Italian peasants of "having nothing in mind but to do as much possible damage to their neighbors, being indifferent church visitors but eager adherents of superstition and witchcraft."

TOWNSMEN

ROME. MID-SEVENTEENTH CENTURY

Rome had deteriorated in every way since the golden days of the Renaissance. Much of the population was destitute and, whether it was true or not, had a reputation for being averse to work. Most of the artisans were foreigners. Thousands of beggars har- assed the passersby, and brigandry in and around the city persisted into the nineteenth century.

These men are dressed for bad weather, the one on the left in a short, circular cape, the other in a large topcoat, tucked up at the waist, with a hood attached.

EXTERMINATOR AND STREET VENDOR

ITALY. MID-SEVENTEENTH CENTURY

With all the vermin that bred on the unsanitary conditions in the towns, you would have expected the exterminator to be an extremely busy person. The fact is that most people simply gave up the fight as hopeless. In the poor districts, houses were often nothing but windowless cubicles where people lived under the same roof as their chickens and pigs. There were still many unpaved roads filled with a deep muck of indescribable composition. It wasn't until the end of the century that we find the first laws against throwing garbage into the streets, but even those were generally ignored.

Blankets worn as cloaks, and the bulbous beret (2) were characteristic garments of Italian laborers.

GONDOLIERS

VENICE. MID-SEVENTEENTH CENTURY

The gondola, the distinctive symbol of Venice, came into existence about 1400. From then on, it served an urgent need for the continuously growing population, as pedestrians and horsemen might otherwise have drowned in the unpaved, mud-covered lanes, and the canals.

By the beginning of the seventeenth century, there were about 10,000 gondolas, some privately owned, some for hire at a regulated fee. At the time of our drawing, gondoliers did not yet wear a special costume, but dressed in simple, comfortable smocks, trousers, and shirts, with a wide-brimmed hat as protection against the weather.

STREET VENDORS
ITALY. MID-SEVENTEENTH CENTURY

The street vendor offers up for sale fans of typical baroque design. His customer is a peasant woman who has brought to market the products of her own vegetable garden. Cabbages, artichokes, eggplants, chestnuts, and all kinds of herbs for the popular raw salads were plentiful and of excellent quality. Other foods sold by itinerant vendors were potatoes, fried fish, and salted meats.

WANDERING HAT MAKER AND CUSTOMER
ITALY, MID-SEVENTEENTH CENTURY

The hatter not only sells but makes his merchandise while walking the streets. All he needs for his creations are two rolls of material, which are attached to his belt, a pair of scissors and a needle and thread. This hatter doesn't have a stall, but if he did it would have a sign made of wood or iron, decorated with a red hat or a black beret instead of a name. Other trades displayed similar signs. A pair of scissors denoted a tailor, a snake meant that the man within was a pharmacist, and a smoking Turk signified tobacconist.

ITINERANT MUSICIAN AND BOY
ITALY. MID-SEVENTEENTH CENTURY

The minstrel and his boy look up at the windows of a wealthy residence, hoping that a few coins will be dropped down. Travelers were constantly impressed by the shocking discrepancy between the splendor of the many palaces and churches and the squalor of the streets, which were populated by beggars, goats, and sheep.

The singer's splendid costume was obviously handed down by some nobleman. It is in the old-fashioned Spanish style.

DESTITUTES

GERMANY. MID-SEVENTEENTH CENTURY

By the end of the Thirty Years War in 1648, many villages in Germany had been turned into rubble or had disappeared completely; the surrounding fields were overgrown with weeds, brush, and nettles. Wherever ruins of houses still stood, they were filled with skeletons of men and women who had been slaughtered or had died of hunger or the plague, and with parts of the carrion of horses and cattle left by the ravens and the wolves. Those peasants who had escaped with their lives wandered over the deserted fields in search of morsels of food. They lived the lives of animals in caves or rude shelters.

Costumes such as these may be seen in a set of anonymous seventeenth-century engravings in the Bibliothèque Nationale in Paris. The best documentation for the life of the common people during and after the Thirty Years War is to be found in the novels of Hans Grimmelshausen.

DESTITUTES

GERMANY. MID-SEVENTEENTH CENTURY

An estimated 15,000 villages in Germany were completely destroyed in the Thirty Years War. In areas which suffered the most, the Palatinate for instance, only one person in ten was said to have survived.

Some of the peasants who did escape with their lives joined up with army stragglers and deserters, forming bands of robbers that roamed the country like packs of hungry wolves.

DOMESTIC SERVANTS
GERMANY. MID-SEVENTEENTH CENTURY

In the seventeenth century it was no trick finding enough servants. Every well-to-do household employed at least three maids, one to cook, one to clean, and one to do the laundry. In addition, some also had a scullery maid and a nursemaid. It was quite another thing, apparently, to find reliable, efficient servants. At least contemporary sources constantly complained about the help's continuous coming and going, calling them slow, lazy, restive, impudent, dirty, negligent, thievish, and so on.

The patterned cap worn by the girl on the left, and the fur hat on the other maid were worn in various regions of Germany. The fur hat became particularly popular in Nuremberg and Augsburg toward the end of the century.

The costumes in this drawing were taken from a leaflet on domestic servants published in Nuremberg in 1652.

TOWNSWOMEN FROM COLOGNE

GERMANY. MID-SEVENTEENTH CENTURY

The mushroom-shaped headpiece worn by the woman on the left consists of a little turned disk and a handle ending in a tuft of wool. It serves to hold the woman's light wrapper in place, and would also similarly be used to anchor a heavy cloak, or Hoike. It was worn all along the Lower Rhine.

The costumes in this drawing show a strong Dutch influence, particularly in the rounded lower border of the bodice. A French bodice, in contrast, would come to a point at the bottom.

BRIDE AND GROOM

ALSACE. MID-SEVENTEENTH CENTURY

A messenger was sent around to invite the guests to a peasant wedding. After the church ceremony, a big meal was served and the maids of honor waited on the bride. This was followed by the traditional dancing and drinking. If the peasants were rich, the feast might last well into the next day, when another celebration would take place for the farm hands and lesser guests.

The bridegroom's mark is the wreath fastened to his hat. His jacket with its padded shoulders is a devel-opment of the old peasant coat. The heavily padded trousers are attached permanently to the stockings.

The bride's distinctive mark is her crown. Other-wise, like her bridegroom, she wears her regular Sun-day costume. Notice her cartwheel collar and the plastron she wears over the front of her shirt. It is made of cardboard and covered with striped cloth, and is a descendant of the medieval armored breast-plate and a relative of a man's starched shirtfront. Her fur-lined jacket, or Kamisol, has puffed shoulders.

TOWNSWOMEN
PARIS. 1650–1700

Women of the people, especially market women, were quick-witted and sharp-tongued, with an inexhaustible vocabulary of epithets, curses, and blasphemies, which they poured on anyone, regardless of station, who aroused their anger.

Both of these women are wearing falling bands, the flat collar of military origin that replaced the Spanish ruff. It was worn by men and women of all classes. Note, too, the early examples of shoes with heels.

The *Cris de Paris*, a collection of drawings of vendors and other street people, was first published in the sixteenth century, and irregularly thereafter. Nicolas Bonnart (1636–1718), whose engravings are the costume source for this drawing, was a prolific contributor to the seventeenth-century editions. In all, there were six engravers by the name of Bonnart in this period, and they were all related.

WOMAN AND BUTCHER
PARIS. 1650–1700

The butchers of Paris constituted a very tightly controlled and influential corporation, and the masterships were restricted to a few families. In theory, each individual butchershop had to be managed by a master butcher. Sometimes, though, the masters, instead of running the business themselves, rented it out to journeymen or other workers who were not even guild members.

The customer in this drawing wears a dress that was typical of a style worn by lower-class women in both town and country. At a time when the dictates of high fashion decreed the pointed bodice, of varying lengths, her bodice is still attached to her skirt in a straight waistline. The bodice is not the same color as the skirt. High-heeled shoes like hers were also worn by men.

CRAFTSMEN
FRANCE. 1650–1700

Craftsmen at their work, or living outside of Paris, rarely dressed "à la mode." The man on the right, for example, is still wearing the old padded trunks.

In the towns the economic conditions were not quite as bad as they were in the country, and most of the time the poor suffered their privations and taxes with considerable patience. But when the edge of starvation was approached, grave uprisings did occur; one of the worst was in 1649.

PEASANTS

FRANCE. 1650–1700

After the tax collector left, not much remained for the peasant except rye and bran to make bread; in the south the bread might have been made of corn and chestnuts. In times of famine, they subsisted on roots and acorns, and had scarcely enough cloth to cover their bare bodies. Along with royal taxes and dues to the seigneur, peasants had to put up with the damage to their property caused by plundering soldiers, as well as by the soldiers who were billeted with them.

Little has changed in rural costume during this century. Wigs, by this time worn in town even by men of the lower classes, never were adopted by the peasants, who stuck to their own hair.

STREET VENDORS
PARIS. 1650–1700

The population of Paris increased from an estimated 30,000 at the beginning of the century to almost 100,000 by 1700. It was a fluctuating population and the newcomers often had a hard time finding work or living accommodations. Still, the people of Paris were less oppressed than those in the provincial towns, not to mention the peasants.

Parisians had no need to go "downtown" for their purchases, because, just as in the sixteenth century, everything was brought to them by innumerable street vendors. The old woman in this drawing is selling old clothes and shoes; her younger companion carries cakes on the tray on her head. Other vendors sold cheese, mustard, fagots, fried and cooked meat, fish, and sausages. Ambulant glaziers, carpenters, and other artisans went from door to door. In addition, there were markets in many parts of the city; the most renowned was in the Rue St. Denis.

LABORERS
ITALY. 1650–1700

Taverns were among the very few recreations available to the poor townsmen. Although the only attractions were wine, simple food, and card games, many men preferred to spend their evenings in a tavern with friends to staying in their poorly lit and furnished homes, eating the monotonous, quickly prepared flour and milk dishes served up by their wives. In Florence,

the wives responded by prevailing upon the city government to forbid the sale of sweets and certain other goodies in the taverns.

Note the one-piece overall worn by the man on the right. This was occasionally seen on laborers in the seventeenth and eighteenth centuries.

PEASANT DANCE

HOLLAND, 1650–1700

Throughout the Middle Ages, the peasant had been considered a funny character, one to be scoffed at for his ugly looks and coarse manner, his sly stupidity, and his dumb pugnacity. To a considerable extent, this continued to be the prevailing attitude. Yet now, in the work of the Dutch Peasant Painters, many of rural origin themselves, we are beginning to see an appreciation of the human qualities of the peasant, hidden under the coarse and often ridiculous exterior.

PEASANT WOMAN AND ORGAN GRINDER

HOLLAND. 1650–1700

The most important event in the life of the rural communities was the country fair. Besides the animals, trained apes and bears, dancing goats, and the singing dog in our drawing, there were performances by jugglers and musicians, rope-dancers, dwarfs, and giants.

Races were held on horses, donkeys, and even cows.

Contests of skill—crossbow target-shooting and, later, riflery—were the main attractions of the festival. All of this activity, of course, went on against a background of eating, drinking, and dancing, sometimes lasting for eight days on end.

BEATERS
ENGLAND. 1650–1700

Both of these men are clad in the early type of coat known as the justaucorps, which evolved out of the old peasant coat by way of the soldier's jerkin of the Thirty Years War. By now it was general wear for men of all classes. It had a closely fitted upper part and a skirt, slit in several places, that reached almost to the knees.

Hats were now stiffer and smaller, and the falling band collar has been replaced by a neckerchief.

BAVARIAN PEASANT AND TOWNSGIRL
GERMANY. LATE SEVENTEENTH CENTURY

We first saw this style of man's shirt early in the century. It was made of wool and cut into two lobes which were folded across the chest. In warm weather, it was worn without a coat, as in this drawing.

The man's other garment of particular significance are his trousers, which start at the knees and end high on his chest, just under the arms. The trousers are laced to the shirt at the top; another set of laces closes the front, and a codpiece is fastened around the hips.

The woman's hat is made of a piece of solid black wood, with a brim of black felt. This headpiece is balanced on top of a hairdo that has been artificially stiffened by an intricate system of quilts and horsehair. Her short cape is a descendant of the Spanish men's cloak, which by now has disappeared from upper-class costume, but which, with a stiffened yoke, is still part of regional costume in this area.

PEASANTS

ENVIRONS OF NUREMBERG. END OF SEVENTEENTH CENTURY

If regional costume was strongly expressed in the holiday outfits we saw in the last drawing, hardly any traces of it can be found in these everyday clothes.

The woman's laced bodice, round peasant skirt, and shoes of the general baroque style, as well as her thick woolen stockings and fur hat, might have been worn by a peasant anywhere in Germany. The same goes for the man's coat, with its shoulder rolls, and his chest covering, as well as all other parts of his costume.

JEWS

VENICE. LATE SEVENTEENTH CENTURY

Space alloted to the ghetto in Venice was limited, so to accommodate the Jewish inhabitants, the buildings had to be unusually tall—as any visitor to that section can still see today. Since artificial light was poor at best, and daylight rarely penetrated the rooms, the Jews, who worked mainly at repairing and cleaning the old clothes in which they traded, suffered from eyestrain and myopia.

Jews still had to wear the yellow ring on a cord around their necks. In 1690, the yellow beret was replaced with a red beret. The cut of the coat on the man to the left still shows the influence of the old oriental caftan.

TOWNSWOMAN AND BAWD
VENICE. END OF SEVENTEENTH CENTURY

The bawd (2) has been employed by some gentle-man to approach the girl for a date. The primary business of these bawds was to lease houses at a low rate and let them out to prostitutes at enormous rents. They also lent money and sold clothes to the girls, again at great profit. Bawds no longer had to dress entirely in yellow, but they did have to wear at least a yellow wrapper.

Women of the people, unlike those of the upper classes, walked through town freely and unaccom-panied. A big kerchief draped around her head and shoulders (1) protected this girl against both weather and unwelcome glances, as well as serving to hide her identity if she so desired. The girl in our drawing is dressed all in black except for her white apron, which is embroidered with green and red flowers.

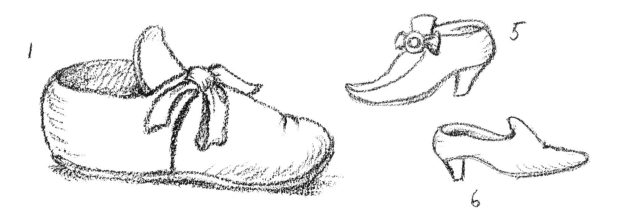

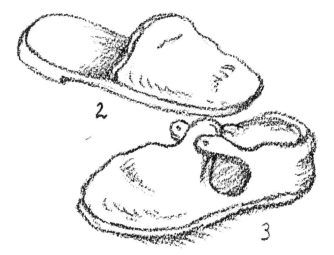

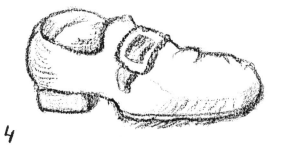

LOWER-CLASS SHOES OF THE SEVENTEENTH AND EIGHTEENTH CENTURIES

1. Artisan's shoe. Seventeenth century.

2. Peasant's slipper, male and female. Seventeenth century.

3. Peasant's shoe, male and female. Seventeenth century.

4. Artisan's shoe, black or brown leather. Eighteenth century.

5. Townswoman's shoe, colored leather or cotton. First half of eighteenth century.

6. Townswoman's shoe, colored leather. Second half of eighteenth century.

7. Servant's slipper, leather or linen. First half of eighteenth century.

8. Artisan's shoe, black leather. Eighteenth century.

Eighteenth Century

PEASANTS FROM LEON

SPAIN. EARLY EIGHTEENTH CENTURY

The inhabitants of the old kingdom of Leon prided
themselves on being of pure Spanish stock (Mara-
gatos), direct descendents of the Visigoths and Celt-
Iberians. As a result, they preserved much of their
old costume, which can be seen in this drawing.

STREET SCENE

MADRID. EIGHTEENTH CENTURY

Spain was the country of greatest social contrasts; poverty in the streets of Madrid was even more noticeable than in other European capitals. The worsening economic situation drove many craftsmen and laborers out of town, but the invalid soldiers and students who did not want to work remained. Beggars physically unable to work were supplied with a license by their parish priests to distinguish them from the "vagos" who could work, but didn't choose to.

Among women of the people, it was still the style to let their tresses dangle down from the tops of their heads.

GARDENER AND LABORER
VALENCIA. EIGHTEENTH CENTURY

Spain was about the only country in Europe where you could still see native costume in the towns, as well as the rural areas. One example of this is the skirtlike apron on the men in this drawing. Even today, although only on festive occasions, this particular native style can be seen in the Canary Islands and certain other regions.

The man on the right wears the small Spanish bicorne. The gardener's Phrygian cap, as well as his sash, were worn in other southern countries as well as Spain. Sandals or shoes fastened to the legs by means of straps were also a typically Spanish style.

STREET VENDORS
MADRID. EIGHTEENTH CENTURY

In the 200 years since the end of its Golden Age, Spain had lost much of its old power and splendor. As poverty increased proportionately, many peasants deserted their houses, which had been completely stripped by the tax collectors, and flocked to the towns. Denied access to the trades and crafts by the guilds, which carefully guarded the rights of their memberships against competition, they tried to make a scanty living as laborers or street vendors.

Like the man from Valencia in the last drawing, this street vendor is wearing the typical Spanish bicorne. The woman's hat also has a Spanish flavor.

TOWNSPEOPLE

PARIS. EARLY EIGHTEENTH CENTURY

At the turn of the century, we find the people of Paris described as saucy and with little reverence for anybody. This spirit produced a kind of elegance of bearing and costume, which often made it impossible, at first glance, to recognize class differences—except, of course, for the very poor.

This man is wearing the typical justaucorps; notice the exceptionally wide cuffs. Beneath it, he wears a very long waistcoat, which is generally sleeveless. His trousers are narrow, almost culottes. His long hair is his own.

The woman's cap is a modest variation of the fontange, a headgear which elegant ladies built up in complicated layers to a height of as much as three or even four feet!

INNKEEPER AND WAITER
FRANCE. EARLY EIGHTEENTH CENTURY

Even though the French usually visited taverns only on Sunday, there were so many of these establishments in Paris, according to a contemporary observer, that their keepers would have populated a good-sized town. Frequently, these tavernkeepers were accused of diluting the wine with water.

The innkeeper, left, wears the waistcoat, which has developed from the doublet. Unlike the long, sleeve-less waistcoat we saw in the last drawing, this one is short, has long sleeves, and is worn without a coat. This garment was popular with all kinds of men of the lower classes.

The innkeeper's baroque shoe, with its long, broad tongue and square toe, is by now giving way to the type of shoe worn by the waiter, without a tongue, with a more pointed toe, and with a lower heel.

PEASANTS

ALSACE. EARLY EIGHTEENTH CENTURY

Regional costume had completely disappeared in the towns, but it was re-emerging in the country. Around the middle of the century, it would fade out here too, once again to come back triumphantly toward the end of the century.

The man on the left is dressed in typically Alsatian Sunday clothes. The costume of his friend, except for the shapeless, big peasant hat, could have been worn by a townsman too.

MEN FROM AVILA AND NAVARRE

SPAIN. EARLY EIGHTEENTH CENTURY

The costume of the man from Navarre, right, shows many regional characteristics. Note especially the wide smock with the laced sleeves and the decorated sleeves of the doublet protruding through the open slits.

The only typically regional garment worn by the man from Avila is his hat.

Not many of the peasants from these regions would have been able to dress this well, since, it is estimated, no more than one out of twenty had an income above the level of poverty.

GLASS BLOWER AND
BOTTLE VENDOR

VENICE. EARLY EIGHTEENTH CENTURY

Every tourist in Venice visits the famous Murano glass factories. In the beginning of the thirteenth century, exquisite samples of Byzantine glass were brought to Venice, where a large number of furnaces were set up to reproduce them. The population, however, rebelled against the fire hazards and the polluted air that the furnaces created, and in 1291 the entire industry was forced to move to the nearby island of Murano. There the glass makers lived almost like exiled prisoners in order to preserve the secrets of the trade.

The glass blower wears a smock of coarse blue wool. His white shirt with its small stand-up collar that could be laced in the front was typical for this period. The woman's costume would be in the dull browns, purples, and rusty reds common to poor people's wear in all ages.

271

"OLD CLOTHES BOUGHT AND SOLD"

ITALY. EARLY EIGHTEENTH CENTURY

Before the days of cheap mass-produced clothes, the purchase of a new garment made a considerable inroad into the family budget. In the towns, therefore, the buying and selling of old clothes was an important factor in the life of the lower classes. Since much of what they bought was the discarded clothing of the upper classes, this meant that to a certain extent, lower-class townspeople kept up with current fashion.

Peasants, on the other hand, rarely had the opportunity, except at the country fairs, to buy recently used clothing. Save for their expensive holiday costumes, their clothes were generally old, abandoned garments, sometimes several generations old. The absence of an old-clothes trade in the country was one of the factors that contributed to the development of rural regional costumes.

In this drawing, the flat, stiff hats worn by the two vendors were typical headwear of common people in various countries during this era.

GONDOLIERS

VENICE, EARLY EIGHTEENTH CENTURY

The annual gondola race on the Grand Canal dates back to the fourteenth century; by the year 1577 there were said to be 8000 gondolas entered in the race.

Traditionally, gondoliers have always sung at their work, usually songs of old Venetian origin, or barcaroles, named after "barcarolo," the Italian word for gondoliers. Frequently the singers combined their songs with snatches of poetry by Torquato Tasso and other poets.

The contestants in one of the eighteenth-century races were dressed like the men in this drawing, who are clad in white shirts, blue breeches, red sashes, white stockings, and black shoes. Their hats would have been red or blue, and the doublet of the man on the left is white with blue trimmings.

NEWFOUNDLAND FISHERMEN

ENGLAND. EARLY EIGHTEENTH CENTURY

One of the early overseas ventures of the English, in the sixteenth century, was fishing for cod along the coast of Newfoundland. The men who fished off those remote shores, along with the herring fishermen who plied the North Sea, played an important role in creating the reservoir of hardy seafaring men who were destined to make England lord of the seas.

The men in our drawing had the job of salting the catch as it was brought on board ship, to preserve it.

COUNTRY WOMEN

FRANCE. 1700–1750

Watteau and his school of painting created a never-never world of carefree shepherds and peasants clad in silk and velvet. But in their preliminary sketches taken from life, some of which served as costume sources for this drawing, these same painters were accurate observers and reporters of the real life of the common people.

These three girls are dressed in the basic components of French lower-class costume of the period, with scarcely any regional characteristics. Bodice and skirt are attached to each other; corsets were worn under the bodice, or sometimes instead of it. Unmarried girls generally wore sleeveless bodices. The skirt was circular and fell in loose folds to the ankles, although sometimes it was worn tucked up. Only in holiday costume do we find pleated skirts. At least one, and often several, petticoats were worn under the skirt.

WOMEN WITH GARBAGE

GERMANY. 1700–1750.

After recovering from the devastation of the Thirty Years War in the seventeenth century, German towns showed many improvements. Cattle were no longer allowed to roam the streets; dungheaps were removed, and the throwing of garbage into the streets, up until now a common practice, was forbidden. Instead, a collecting service was set up, for which these two women are waiting.

In the towns, regional costume reached its highest development in the seventeenth century. By now it had vanished almost completely. All classes all over Europe followed the line of French fashions.

CAKE VENDORS

ENGLAND. 1725–1750

William Hogarth, who lived from 1697 to 1764, was one of the few painters outside of Holland to break away from the baroque style of painting, which considered heroes and saints the only subjects worth preserving in oil. By employing a moralizing tone—*The Rake's Progress* and *The Harlot's Progress*—to gain the interest of the English middle class, Hogarth depicted the life of the people of London, including the lower classes. With keen observation and deep understanding, he created an almost complete register of their characters. Hogarth's paintings are my source for this and several of the following drawings.

SHOW PEOPLE

ENGLAND. 1725–1750

Fairs were a popular form of entertainment with people of all classes of society, who flocked to them from all over, even from quite distant towns. Some of the festivals lasted a week or longer. Besides the puppet and peep shows, whose operators we see in this drawing, there were wandering actors and musicians, all kinds of acrobats and jesters, and quacks and freaks to entertain the people.

SHOW PEOPLE
ENGLAND. 1725–1750

In addition to the fairs, there were permanent places of amusement in London. The best known were Vauxhall, the Pantheon, and Marylebone Gardens, where nobles and commoners mixed freely.

The woman drummer is wearing mouches, or black beauty marks, on her face. Although these were fancied by society women, among the lower classes only show people and prostitutes wore them.

Show business was no exception to the practice among virtually all enterprises of exploiting child labor; even children as young as six years old were put to work for the benefit of their elders.

BALLAD SINGERS

ENGLAND. 1725–1750

Ballad singers, like the girl in this drawing, as well as other entertainers, could be found on street corners, in addition to the established places of entertainment. Here she recites to the tune of her companion's fiddle, then sells copies of her ballads to the public. The theme of her song might be the tale of Robin Hood, a popular version of a classic myth, or a song about a recent happening, preferably the life, loves, and death of a famous highwayman. These ballads were usually the only kind of literature that the common people had.

PROSTITUTES

ENGLAND. 1725–1750

The streets of London and other English towns and cities swarmed with prostitutes. A crackdown on the notorious Alsatia, a London quarter inhabited almost exclusively by harlots, pimps, thieves, and other criminals, simply had the effect of scattering the prostitutes to all of the other parts of the city, with the result that many quarters were now dangerous for decent women after dark.

The ranks of the prostitutes were constantly replenished with girls who had been seduced and with unmarried mothers who were repudiated by their families. A contributing factor was the difficulty women experienced in finding a way to make a decent living on their own.

COACHMAN AND CARTER

ENGLAND. 1725-1750

By the second quarter of the century, the stage-coach was an established institution, although travel-ing in one was anything but comfortable. Drawn by four or six horses, and with no springs, the coaches frequently overturned on the roads, still largely in deplorable condition. Moreover, the risk of being held up by a highwayman was as great as ever.

The man on the left was either the driver of a private coach or a stagecoach. His greatcoat was a favorite garment with coachmen. In general, topcoats were rarely worn by the common men of the eight-eenth century, who protected themselves against bad weather by wearing several layers of underwear, a waistcoat, and the justaucorps. The carter, right, is wearing a smock in a style that dates back to ancient days.

COMMONERS AT A PARTY

ENGLAND. 1725–1750

In an era when manners, at best, were rather boisterous, parties easily got out of hand. According to a contemporary description, "one guzzled like horses and then one started to dance and to scatter one's wigs, hats, and coats."

Wigs had appeared on the fashion scene in the middle of the seventeenth century. Except for certain professional people, such as physicians and lawyers, the common man never used the long, full wig. If he wasn't wearing only his own hair, long and combed back in the current fashion, he wore a small wig made of horse or goat hair. Blond or brown wigs were more expensive than the black ones, which were usually powdered.

The man on the left balances his wig on his cane. His companion's headpiece has slipped across his forehead; the front is over his right ear.

SAILOR AND INNKEEPER

ENGLAND. 1725–1750

The invalid sailor has no intention of paying his bill, probably because he isn't able to. The situation of soldiers and sailors out of service is best illustrated by the fact that they were legally allowed to beg even if they were not incapacitated. The sailor wears the typical costume of men of his occupation—small tricorne, jerkin, neckerchief, and the loose trousers that just reach the tops of his thick woolen socks.

The bill presented by the angry innkeeper probably is for a meal of meat and pickles in a sharp sauce, bread, and ale or gin. During the first decades of the century, gin began to rival beer as the common people's drink, and was credited with contributing to a sharp rise in the death rate.

JOURNEYMAN AND CUSTOMER
ALSACE. 1725–1750

The guilds, which came to life after the Thirty Years War, were still strong enough to resist the rising tide of industrialism. Although many venerable old customs and ceremonies, such as the formal promotion from apprentice to journeyman, were discarded, the actual practices were not. The apprentice still had to undergo from two to six years of virtual servitude, and the journeyman had to wander for another three to five years from one town to another in search of work. If, in his wandering, he happened to stray into one

of the many territories into which Germany was partitioned, one that also happened to be out of bounds for citizens of his region, he would very likely end up serving a sentence in a dingy prison.

The jacket on the woman customer is in a style that has become an integral part of lower-class dress. In Germany and Austria it was known under various names, such as Kamisol, Leibel, Rockel, and Joppen. In France, where it was called the camisole, it was the predecessor of the fashionable caraco.

TRAVELING PHYSICIAN AND HOUSEWIFE

FRANCE. 1725–1750

Ambulant physicians and town physicians were considered quite separate members of the medical profession. As early as the sixteenth century, physicians went up and down the streets offering their services. When they traveled across country, they rode on a horse or a mule, often accompanied by an assistant and a pack animal, so that they formed quite a formidable entourage.

According to contemporary sources, the town physicians were so overworked that they could devote no more than a quarter of an hour to a patient. Although their working day began at five in the morning, and lasted for nineteen hours, they still had to use lunchtime to write their prescriptions.

The chain slung around the doctor's body is made up of boxes containing medications.

PRINT VENDOR AND CUSTOMER
GERMANY. MID-EIGHTEENTH CENTURY

With the improvement of printing techniques, cheap prints of landscapes, rare animals, and other subjects were now mass-produced and available to pretty nearly anybody.

The kind of nightcap worn by the vendor was quite popular in Germany among workingmen as a change from the tricorne, which remained the dominant style. Stockings were now generally tucked under the breeches, and men like our vendor, who had to spend their days outdoors, frequently strapped gaiters on top of them for better protection.

SHOW PEOPLE
GERMANY. MID-EIGHTEENTH CENTURY

The man in this drawing comes from the East, or at least fancies a costume of Eastern flavor, which was not uncommon among show people. Here, he is giving a running commentary on a series of pictures—the illustrated story is probably a very gory tale of murder.

The woman sells leaflets with the same story printed on them. The leaflets were very often illustrated, and as far as they have been preserved, provide a rare source of information about the costumes of the lower classes. In our illustration, the woman is clad in garments worn by the very poorest class of people.

PEASANT GIRLS

ENVIRONS OF SAXONY AND AUGSBURG. MID-EIGHTEENTH
CENTURY

The Saxon girl, left, is dressed in her holiday outfit.
Her bonnet, known as a Schniepen, is strongly
regional and a most remarkable affair, with long,
sharp edges that grip her forehead and cheeks in the
manner of a claw.

The everyday costume on the girl from Augsburg
shows no regional distinctions.

BOATMEN

GERMANY. MID-EIGHTEENTH CENTURY

Facilities for traveling by road were still poor, partly because many of the dozen governments of Germany operated on the theory that bad roads prevented people from traveling and therefore kept their money in the country. As a result, those who did travel found that going by water offered a welcome alternative to a bumpy land journey. On some sections of the Rhine and the Danube there were quite comfortable boats to be found.

EMIGRANT PEASANTS

AUSTRIA. MID-EIGHTEENTH CENTURY

These peasants are headed for America. There were always sufficient reasons, but not so many possibilities, to emigrate. The situation of the Austrian peasants was no better than that of any other Germans. In addition, the small pockets of Protestant communities that had survived purges in past centuries still suffered from sporadic persecution and discrimination.

The man and woman in this drawing are from the Austrian Alps. Their jackets are made of loden cloth, but the man's pants, typically, are of leather. The basic colors of the costumes are greens and grays, and occasionally browns, but decorations and trimmings are likely to be in all colors of the rainbow.

TOWNSFOLK

FRANCE. MID-EIGHTEENTH CENTURY

Ruthless taxation, inflation, and a series of bad harvests had shaken the paternal relationship between the king and the people of France. The loyal, conservative artisan has, to a degree, been replaced by the industrial worker. The latter, often with his wife and children, had to slave for fourteen or more hours a day in the mill to extract a meager living. This oppressed working class was a group ripe for rebellion, and many small uprisings occurred here and there before the big revolution.

The man and his wife shown here belong to a very poor level of society, to judge from his clothes, in particular. The wife, incidentally, displays considerably more revolutionary ardor than her spouse.

SERVANT GIRLS
FRANCE, MID-EIGHTEENTH CENTURY

Except for their miserable housing conditions, servant girls in the eighteenth century were often very well off. They got a reasonably good salary, in addition to which they stood to make extra money on the side while doing the marketing.

Domestic servants in this era were better dressed than the average housewife of a few decades ago. Caps and bonnets had a run of popularity; two of the many variations are worn here by the chambermaid, left, and the cook, just returned from shopping.

Both of the servants are wearing the caraco, a form of jacket developed from the camisole, see page 285. The outfits on these women would have been very colorful—white caps decorated with colored ribbons, the caracos yellow or reddish brown, the skirts red or blue, aprons and stockings white, and shoes black, brown, or beige. Printed calicos and cottons, which had been very expensive, could now be had most reasonably, and even women of modest means could use these materials.

CATERER AND STREET VENDOR

VENICE. MID-EIGHTEENTH CENTURY

This and the next few drawings are based on the work of Giovanni Grevenbroeck II, who lived from 1731 to 1801. He was a Dutch artist living in Venice, who did work for the government as well as private institutions. Among his works were a series of watercolor sketches of Venetian costume from the sixteenth century to his own time. (His sketches of the earlier costumes were mostly copied from the work of Titian, the greatest of the Venetian painters.)

Although Grevenbroeck's artistic ability cannot be compared with such other artists of the same subject as Longhi, Guardi, or Canaletto, his collection is one of the most comprehensive studies of the appearance of the common people of a given place and time. This collection can be seen in the library of the Museo Correr, the city museum of Venice, or in reproduction in the Centro Internazionale delle Arti e del Costume in the Palazzo Grassi, also in Venice.

LOTTERY TICKET VENDOR
AND PAVER

VENICE. MID-EIGHTEENTH CENTURY

The terrazaro, or paver, got his name from a particular mixture of ingredients popularly used for paving floors, known as terrazo. Paving, both indoors and out, was a most important job in Venice, and the pavers' guild, with San Florian Martire as its patron saint, was a highly respected one.

The name of the paver, right in our drawing, is being entered into the register of the ticket vendor as a participant in the next raffle. Samples of the possible winnings are exhibited on the board which is attached to the vendor's belt.

LAMPLIGHTER AND KEEPER OF BOXES

VENICE. MID-EIGHTEENTH CENTURY

By the beginning of the eighteenth century, Venice had a reasonably good system of street lighting, in contrast to other Italian cities that had only an occasional lamp in a few streets. In Spain, the only street light often came from the little oil lamps in front of the pictures of saints at the street corners. Conditions were a little better in England, France, and parts of Germany.

The man on the right is keeper of the keys to the theatrical boxes belonging to noble families. He made extra money on the side by renting out the unused boxes. His circular cape took the place of a topcoat.

ALMS COLLECTORS

VENICE. MID-EIGHTEENTH CENTURY

The two artisans are collecting contributions for the church of the patron saint either of their guild or town quarter. One tunes up his fiddle to attract the attention of passersby, while the other holds up a statue of the saint.

Both men are dressed in everyday clothes; the man on the right has probably just stepped out of his shop. Their costume, as well as the way the saint's image is merely hoisted aloft on an amateurishly decorated ring on a pole, indicates that this was just an ordinary day. Had it been the saint's day or some other festive occasion, altars would have been set up about town, with rich ornamentation detailing the story of the saint's martyrdom, and confraternities would have performed on colorful stages, erected for that purpose.

WATER VENDOR

MADRID. MID-EIGHTEENTH CENTURY

In Madrid, as in Rome and most other European cities, there was a scarcity of fresh pure water. Drinking water was brought into town and sold in the streets, and those well-to-do citizens who lived on the upper floors of the houses hired men to carry it upstairs.

With the possible exception of their hats and the short jacket worn by the man on the left, the costume of these two men from Madrid is not peculiar to their region.

PEASANTS

PORTUGAL. MID-EIGHTEENTH CENTURY

Despite the leveling trend of the eighteenth century, under which many of the regional peculiarities of lower-class dress disappeared in Europe, we still find many traces of national costume. In Portugal, as shown here, these are the man's red smock, buttoned down the front, his flat hat, and his long cape of a heavy dark material, lined in white.

The woman's bodice is olive green, her two skirts (one tucked up) are brown, as is the piece of cloth draped over her head and shoulders. Her head is wrapped in a white kerchief, a corner of which falls over her left shoulder. Her shirt, of which only the cuffs are visible, is also white.

FARMER AND PICKPOCKET

ENGLAND. MID-EIGHTEENTH CENTURY

Many a farmer, who in earlier days would have lived his entire life without ever leaving the country, now, with improved transport, went to a visit to "fabulous" London. When he got there, alas, he often met up with some most unwelcome experiences, as witness the poor farmer in this drawing.

The number of beggars in the streets of London was still a public disgrace, and many of them got their main income from picking pockets. They were apparently not deterred by the fact that even minor thefts were punishable by death, especially if the crime involved stealing some object, be it only a handkerchief, from a person's body. On the other hand, with hardly any police force in existence, the odds of getting away with it were in favor of the criminal. Even if he was caught, he had a good chance of getting off the hook with the aid of a good lawyer, supplied by the gangs.

WAITER AND TRAVELER
ENGLAND. MID-EIGHTEENTH CENTURY

Quite wisely, the traveler keeps an eye on his bags and packages as he waits outside the inn for the stage coach. In those days, stage coaches had inside seats for only six passengers. Those who rode outside had to accommodate themselves on the roof with the luggage.

Our traveler is wrapped in a warm greatcoat, similar to that of the coachman in the drawing on page 282, but with a different collar.

The waiter wears a hat characteristic of his trade, and no wig, which was expressly forbidden to a waiter. He has tied an apron over a type of comfortable jacket which had made its appearance among working-men of several countries. In France, this jacket was known as the carmagnol; in Austria is was the Spenzer.

PHYSICIANS

ENGLAND. MID-EIGHTEENTH CENTURY

Physicians wore elaborate full-length wigs as a mark of their profession, although, except for a few celebrities, most of them were not of very elevated social standing. Doctors were among Hogarth's favorite subjects, and his feelings toward them apparently were far from benevolent.

Just as in the Middle Ages, the patient's urine was still the main source for a diagnosis and, as we can see in this drawing, two doctors rarely arrived at the same conclusion from looking at the same sample.

MARKET PEOPLE
LONDON. MID-EIGHTEENTH CENTURY

For some reason, English lower-class women, especially those who worked in the markets, liked to wear their hats back to front. Working clothes were dull and unobtrusive in color, mainly browns, purples, and grays; women sometimes wore reds or yellows, too. The materials were wool and coarse linen. On Sundays, women preferred serge and liked their aprons made of a finer linen.

The man in this drawing has negligently tucked his right leather stocking under his trousers and pulled the left stocking over the trousers, where he has fastened it by a ribbon below the knee. Either way was possible at this time, although men working out of doors usually preferred the latter. Knitted stockings were the general rule, but some laborers still wore stockings cut from leather or wool and sewn together.

TOWNSPEOPLE

NAPLES. 1750–1775

In the south of Italy, where any kind of progress was blocked by a long-established and outmoded regime, poverty was most extreme. Public safety, everywhere at a low level, was at its lowest here, where the people sided wholeheartedly with the bandits against the military.

Yet with it all, the rigors of life were somewhat mitigated by the climate, which was pleasant for most of the year, making it possible to spend much of the day and night outdoors enjoying the weather and the beautiful scenery.

WOMAN FROM POZZUOLI AND
MAN FROM NAPLES

ITALY. 1750–1775

The boatman is not very happy with his fare. Still, if we trust contemporary descriptions, it was probably adequate for the kind of service rendered. The boats for passenger use were uncomfortable and dirty, but still preferable to the roads, which were almost impassable.

The lower classes in the Kingdom of Naples were very poor and the costume of the poorest often con-sisted of nothing but rags. Just the same, it was extremely colorful, and set against a colorful back-ground—churches were painted in gay colors, as were coaches and boats; deep reds prevailed and there was lots of tinsel, even on the legs of lamb for sale in the butcher shops. Women's dress in particular displayed an unlimited variety of vivid colors.

BEAR TRAINER AND ASSISTANT

ITALY. 1750–1800

Note the similarity in the costume worn by the man leading the bear to that of the German entertainer, page 288. Fairs continued to be held in all Italian towns, and a permanent one was housed at the Riva in Venice, where animal trainers and acrobats competed with the actors of the Commedia dell'arte. Because of the disposition of the people, renowned as it was for its sweetness, the well-organized police rarely had cause to intervene by force.

SAILOR AND PEASANT GIRL

GENOA. 1750–1800

Genoa had replaced Venice as Italy's leading sea power and her marines were considered among the best in Europe. The sailor in this drawing is wearing the Phrygian cap and wide trousers that are typical costume for seafaring men of this period.

From her dress, the peasant girl could come from any part of Italy. The color of her corselet was probably red and her skirt blue. We would find the same colors, incidentally, in the man's costume: the stripes of his shirt red or blue, the cap red, and the trousers of unbleached linen or natural canvas.

MASKED CITIZEN AND BEGGAR
VENICE. 1750–1800

The protective anonymity afforded by wearing a mask was not only convenient for the well-to-do citizen, but also for a group of beggars known as the "bashful poor." During the carnival, the beggars hid their identity behind their masks in order to place themselves close to the most-frequented parts of the city. Once they maneuvered themselves there, they were careful to display their official begging permits. Without these, they were liable to be sent to the workhouse or to forced labor rowing on the galleys.

PEASANTS OF THE PO PLAINS
ITALY. 1750–1800

The lack of capital and equipment to care for their rice fields properly caused much hardship to the peasants of the plains of Lombardy and Venetia. Even so, they were not quite as poor as the peasants who lived farther south, where some regions were completely isolated because neither the roads nor the bridges were maintained. Many of these peasants lacked everything beyond the barest necessities for living: they had almost no furniture for their houses, were ill-clad, and poorly nourished.

PEASANTS

SICILY. 1750–1800

Of all of the sections of the Kingdom of Naples, which suffered from an administration that was bad beyond description, Sicily was the poorest. Outside the towns, there were few roads other than mule paths, and travelers who had to spend a night on the road usually passed it in a stable or within the crumbling walls of some deserted building.

These peasants are in their Sunday best, which appears poor enough. The stripes of the woman's corselet, worn over a bodice, are in local colors, mostly reds or blues. Her sleeves, although made of a different material, would be the same colors.

The boy's costume, including his hat and the blanket that serves as his cloak, is in the general Italian style. On workdays, he was probably dressed in rags; the woman would have worn an old dress of black serge and a woolen corselet. A husband and wife often shared a single blanket.

PEASANTS

TIROL. 1750–1800

Except in a few regions along the North Sea, the only German-speaking peasants to remain free were the Swiss, the Tirolese, and some of the Austrian Styrians.

The Tirolese were tough mountaineers and deer hunters, ruled by a fierce loyalty to the Catholic faith and their emperor. This would come to a test in the year 1809, at a time when Napoleon held Europe in an iron grip, when they would rise up against him and, armed only with rifles and scythes, temporarily drive the French and their Bavarian allies out of the country.

The style of costume generally known as Tirolean achieved its full development only at the end of the eighteenth century. Even before, however, it had a strong character of its own, expressed here in the hats and loden jackets, in the man's apronlike vest, and the woman's bodice and skirt.

TOWNSWOMEN

GERMANY. 1750–1800

There were, of course, distinctions between the way the upper-class nobility and the commoners dressed. But there were equally sharp differences between commoners of the upper, middle, and lower classes, backed by sumptuary laws. For example, the wives and daughters of craftsmen and laborers, as well as serving women, were not supposed to wear velvet or silk or certain furs. If they publicly displayed gold or silver ornaments or embroidery on any part of their clothing, the bailiffs were instructed to tear off the offending objects. Likewise, lower-class women were not supposed to lace and stiffen their bodices to the same degree that their betters did; instead they simply inserted some whalebone either in front or back.

LAUNDRESSES

GERMANY. 1750–1800

Since washday threw the whole household into turmoil, it is probably just as well that it occurred at infrequent intervals, sometimes only once every three or four months.

Even the ordinary day's work of an eighteenth-century housewife and her servants was considerable— making and repairing clothes; baking bread, preserving fruits and other food; constantly carrying wood or coal from the cellar to keep the stoves hot; fetching water from often quite remote fountains; shopping every day and going from store to store for each single item. Now add to this the enormous amount of work on laundry day, when the weeks' accumulation of clothes for a big family had to be washed, dried, and ironed inside, you can imagine the mood of the women of the house!

Caps had made their appearance at the end of the seventeenth century, and now were worn by all married townswomen, including servants. Although they came in a variety of shapes, they were all of the same basic style: a small crown surrounded by a frilled brim, and decorated with colored ribbons. Unmarried girls usually went bareheaded, even outdoors.

MASON AND MAN FROM SEGOVIA

SPAIN. 1750–1800

Outside of the towns, only the houses in mountainous regions were built of stone. In the plains, they were constructed of clay and straw. The mason, left, is wearing a bicorne and a jacket, with the long sleeves laced to it, and laced shoes that are all in the general Spanish style.

Castilians, known for their pride and grave grandezza, were rigidly conservative. This quality is expressed in the costume on the man from Segovia, which dates back to the seventeenth century.

314

PEASANTS FROM ARAGON AND BILBAO

SPAIN. 1750–1800

It was in Aragon that the seignorial power fell most repressively on the peasants. Their condition was so desperate that many of them joined the "Germania," a far-flung organization of robbers and murderers from all parts of Spain. Although mostly concentrated in the cities, where they often worked hand in glove with the police, their activities also extended to sparsely inhabited, preferably mountain-ous, rural regions which offered good hideouts.

The costumes on these men, who live in different provinces, are virtually identical; neither shows any regional characteristics. The cross-gartering of the legs dates back to the Middle Ages, and, except in parts of Italy and the Iberian peninsula, has long been outmoded in Europe.

WOMEN FROM MURCIA, BILBAO, AND ARAGON

SPAIN. 1750–1800

Urban dress, even in individualistic Spain, followed the French mode rather than national or regional styles. Just like women in Italy and Germany, the girl from Bilbao, center, is wearing the French jacket known as the caraco, and a hoop skirt.

Native dress was more likely to be found in the coun-try, in peasant costume. Here are some examples in the headgear of the girl from Murcia, left, and in the stand-up collar of the girl from Aragon. This Spanish collar, known as a golilla, had once been a popular fashion with women throughout Europe.

PEASANTS

DENMARK. 1750–1800

Nowhere did peasant costume show more infinite regional variety than in the Scandinavian countries, where it differed from parish to parish. It is impossible to give here more than an occasional example.

The girl in this drawing is dressed to go to church. Note the old Spanish influence on her collar and on the cuffs of the man's coat.

PEASANTS

ICELAND. 1750–1800

Even in this remote outpost of Europe, we can find similarities between the dress of peasants in different countries. Thus, the man's suspenders are typical of those worn by men in Bavaria and many regions of the Alps. The woman's ruff, which went out of style a hundred years ago, could still be found in various parts of Germany. Her peculiar hat, which could also have been seen in some Spanish and Italian localities, probably dates back to the French Burgundian henin of the Middle Ages. Metal ornaments similar to those on her belt remind us of the ones worn by Frisian women.

PEASANT WOMEN
SWEDEN. 1750–1800

Each of these women wears several skirts; the longest and narrowest on the inside, the shortest and fullest on top. The cloak of the woman on the left is a relative of the Dutch-German hoike. The colors of their clothes are predominantly red and yellow, and the border decorations are typically Swedish.

WOMEN FROM DANZIG AND WURTEMBERG

GERMANY. 1775–1800

The woman from Danzig, left, wears a short shirt with flaps crossed over her breast under the laced bodice. Strong hooks attached to the bodice hold up the skirt and petticoats. As protection against the weather, she wears a small woolen cape, trimmed with fur. Her bonnet, made of black or brown straw, is in a style then popular among women in northeast Germany. Later it will be worn by women throughout the country.

The costume on the woman from Wurtemberg is not local, but typical of lower-class German fashion toward the end of the eighteenth century.

PEASANTS

ENVIRONS OF NUREMBERG AND BERLIN. 1775–1800

The peasant from Nuremberg is considerably more elegant than the girl from Berlin. Partly this is because he is in his Sunday best (although he would wear a similar coat on weekdays, too) and she is dressed for work, but actually the difference goes deeper than that. For centuries, Nuremberg had been one of the richest cities in Germany, with a high standard of living that found its expression even in the costume of the peasant. Berlin, on the contrary, was still an upstart among German cities and its inhabitants lived and dressed in a Spartan manner.

The girl's skirt could be red or green, her neckerchief of printed wool or cotton. In the warm season, peasant women generally went barefoot, saving their stockings for holidays. The coarse straw hat this girl is wearing is similar to the one we saw in the last drawing on the woman from Danzig.

ARTISAN AND WIFE

GERMANY. 1775–1800

The life of the artisan was still regulated by his guild, from the time of his admission until his death. A new master was limited to one workshop and one apprentice. Tailors were never allowed to employ more than four journeymen. Apprentices had to take a solemn oath to settle eventually in their own town and to teach the craft to no one but the children of that town.

The young artisan is dressed in his everyday clothes. However, he would not wear even his holiday clothes for an official occasion, such as a guild meeting, a reception, a procession, or the like. The costume worn by the guild officers and members on such occasions was strictly ceremonial and unrelated to everyday or even holiday dress. As in the case of military uniforms, it does not fall within the scope of this book.

The wife's jacket, or negligé, was originally worn only in the house or in bed. Later it would be worn in public, too.

TOWNSFOLK

GERMANY. 1775–1800

Watching (and then criticizing) one's neighbors was a favorite pastime among townspeople of the eighteenth century. Women, especially, watched each other suspiciously to see that they did not display finery or other marks of luxury reserved for the upper classes. Some of them, it was reported, actually resorted to violence to remove the objectionable articles from the offender's person.

The most important part of the man's costume is his frock coat. The change from justaucorps to the frock coat, for townsmen of all classes, took place after the middle of the century. Like so many of the earlier changes in men's costume, this one could also be traced to the soldier. Army officers objected to the narrow long coat, with skirts that hampered freedom of movement. At first they just turned back the troublesome parts, then they cut them off.

Note the longer sleeves on the frock coat, and the shorter waistcoat than those we have seen before.

PEASANTS

GERMANY. 1775–1800

Although within a few decades after the Thirty Years War, the German peasants had pretty much recovered from the war's terror and damage, a century later they were still oppressed by unmitigated serfdom. They still had to perform compulsory labor on the lord's land a certain number of days a week. They still had to pay long lists of dues and taxes, including the ancient duty of having to deliver up the best head of cattle on the death of the head of the peasant family.

The peasants in the Electorate of Saxony and in Thuringia were comparatively well off; in fact they were virtually free men. Those in East Prussia were worst off; according to contemporary reports, some of them preferred death to the life they were forced to lead.

PEASANTS FROM BADEN

GERMANY. 1775–1800

In Baden, personal services to the lord were comparatively limited and serfdom manifested itself mainly in the paying of rent. Even some crafts in the villages were open to bonded men, and the man in this drawing might be not only a peasant but perhaps also a tailor, a carpenter, or a weaver.

His wide and loose justaucorps, without a waistline or front fastenings, resembles in shape the old peasant coat, from which it stems. In winter it would be made of black wool or ribbed velvet, and lined in a material of a different color. In summer it was made of white unlined linen.

The woman's jacket imitates the fashion in town and is stiffened with whalebones. She wears a man's hat.

PEASANTS FROM BAVARIA

GERMANY. 1775–1800

The peasants of Upper Bavaria, which today is an important tourist center, were among the poorest in all of Germany, unable to take proper care of their own farms or those of the landowner.

This couple from the Allgäu valley are dressed for the rough weather of the mountains. The man's raincoat is made of two pieces of heavy loden cloth sewn together at the shoulders; it also serves him as a blanket. Although he could probably neither read nor write, those letters on either side of the slit at the neck are his initials. In other regions, two little red hearts took the place of the initials.

The woman's circular wrapping is also made of loden cloth. Her stockings can be stretched, accordion-like, to double their length. Stockings like this were worn in various sections of the Alps.

OIL VENDOR AND TOWNSMAN
NAPLES. 1775–1800

More and more workingmen in Italian cities were being absorbed as laborers into the growing industries, which were coming to replace the old workshops. Still, some artisans, especially those doing fine work in leather, wood, and jewelry, kept up their traditional corporations.

The kerchief tied over the head and topped by a hat were characteristic headgear of the common man throughout southern Europe. So, too, was the sash we see here on the townsman. The olive oil, which is being dispensed by the vendor, was one of the most important components of Neapolitan diet and commerce.

TUSCAN COUNTRY GIRL AND
WOMAN OF FLORENCE

ITALY. 1775–1800

The girl bringing a hen to market is dressed in the usual Italian manner. She has fastened a padded roll around her hips under her skirt—the lower-class woman's equivalent of the hoop skirt.

The townswoman wears the Florentine type of straw hat. Her broad upturned sleeves reveal fine pleated shirt sleeves, and her small hooped skirt is in the general fashion of the day. Muffs are occasionally worn in most European cities.

PEASANT WOMEN WITH PRODUCE

ENVIRONS OF VENICE. 1775–1800

Palestrina, Chioggia, and other villages around Venice abounded in gardens, orchards, and vineyards. The women of the villages regularly transported the excellent fruits and vegetables from their gardens to the city markets.

The woman on the left wears a laced corset under her sleeveless vest, which is stiffened with whalebones and comes to a point in the front. Like most Italian peasant girls, she goes barefoot most of the year, even when decked out in her best clothes.

The woman on the right is wearing a jacket similar to the French caraco, and no corset. Venetian women liked to wear several petticoats under their skirts.

PATRON AND BOATSMAN

VENICE. 1775–1800

It was common practice to expect, or ask for, a tip for any small service rendered. Thus, it was said of customs officials in Milan that they requested a tip from travelers instead of opening their bags. The cobbler who mended a pair of shoes expected a tip in addition to his fee, and the man on the street who was asked for directions also expected a reward.

The man on the left, wearing the sailor's hat, is robed in a long woolen cloak. That same cloak, when worn by a member of the upper classes, would have been made of taffeta.

The closely fitted short jacket (or long-sleeved vest) on the other man is one we have seen on working-men of other countries during the eighteenth century.

TOWNSWOMEN

ITALY. 1775–1800

Married Italian women of the lower classes enjoyed a certain limited amount of freedom, although without their husbands they scarcely left the surroundings of their homes except to go to church. Young girls, even when they were engaged, were not allowed to go for the shortest walk with their fiancés without a chaperon. They were never allowed to go to dances.

As women began to enter the growing industries, the rules became somewhat more relaxed. Upper-class women never observed them as strictly as did women of the lower classes.

The woman on the right, a member of the middle class, wears a small hoop under her long petticoat.

PEOPLE FROM BRABANT

NETHERLANDS. 1775–1800

The Spanish farthingale, a hoop of heavy construction and quite enormous dimensions, which had once dominated European female fashion, went out of style in the beginning of the seventeenth century. However, it never quite disappeared in Spain or in countries that had been under Spanish domination, and it reappeared in a somewhat changed shape in England around the beginning of the eighteenth century, quickly to spread all over Europe. It was originally too expensive for poor people, until cheaper methods of production were invented.

The woman in this drawing is wearing a hoop of quite respectable size under her skirts. Her small, pointed hat has long been popular, in one style or another, with people of the Netherlands.

On top of his long, belted smock, the man is wearing one of those typical workingman's jackets we have seen in various countries.

PEASANTS FROM THE ANGOUMOIS

FRANCE. 1775–1800

As the century drew to a close, the situation of the peasantry was no better; in fact, it had even deteriorated when compared to certain periods of prosperity during the seventeenth century. Peasants still represented about two thirds of the population, and on the peasants' shoulders rested the main burden of governmental taxes, in addition to the dues and services owed the seigneur. Prerevolution literature describes the peasants as "miserable slaves" and "comparable only to draught animals." At some castles, as many as two hundred peasants came begging in a day.

SHEPHERD, ENVIRONS OF BORDEAUX, AND GIRL FROM ROCHELLE

FRANCE. 1775–1800

The shepherd's heavy woolen cape with its jagged hemline and his stockings with notched borders are both regional to his area as well as indicators of his profession. The long staff served as a prop when he walked on stilts across the marshy pastures. (His stilts, unlike those used by children and circus entertainers, were strapped to the soles of his feet.)

The girl wears the commode, a pillow attached under the skirt above the seat. It was both more comfortable and cheaper than the hoop skirt, and therefore usually preferred by lower-class women. The commode is similar to, but not to be confused with, the cul de Paris, a similarly placed pillow, that did not appear until the nineteenth century.

Peasant colors were blues, browns, and purplish reds. Stripes were usually blue and white.

PEASANTS
BOHEMIA. 1775–1800

The man's wide trousers, which we have seen on peasants of other areas in this period, date back to the sixteenth and seventeenth centuries. The shoes on both of these people are also of an old-fashioned design, as, indeed, are most parts of the woman's costume.

Regional to Bohemia are the man's hat and suspenders and the woman's headcovering. This last is a triangularly folded kerchief with two side corners crossed and tied behind the back, then pulled up and forward. At the end of the eighteenth and in the first half of the nineteenth century, the combination of retained roccoco and Biedermeier elements with regional peculiarities created what we have come to think of as European peasant costume. Contrary to popular belief, such costume did not originate in the distant past. See also page 337.

TRAVELERS

GERMANY. 1775–1800

This middle-class woman is wearing a commode, like the one on the French girl we saw in a previous drawing. Her whole figure is covered by a loosely fitting gown, or manteau, a style made popular by Mme. de Maintenon, the mistress and later wife of Louis XIV. The manteau also appeared in variations known as adrienne, hollandaise, or, most often, contouche. Only a small part of her stiffly lined petticoat is visible.

Her traveling hat is perched on top of her hairdo, which is a moderate version of the spectacular coiffure of Marie Antoinette's day. Although not a wig, that style was built up to its enormous proportions by means of false hair and padding. Middle-class women couldn't afford the time or money to renew even their modest versions of this coiffure very often, which was not very conducive to cleanliness.

The man's greatcoat is similar to ones we have seen on men in England.

PEASANTS
BAVARIA. 1775–1800

The man's coat is in the shape of the old justau-corps, which by now is out of style in town. His sus-penders, belt, and hat are characteristic for his region. None of his wife's costume is typically Bavarian, but might have been seen on any lower-class German woman.

Regional peasant costume, which we have seen in the sixteenth and seventeenth centuries, and in the first decades of the eighteenth, had pretty much dis-appeared in the second half of the century. Rural costume now does not differ much from that worn in cities. It started a new revival at the very end of the century.

WURTEMBERG PEASANTS IN MOURNING

GERMANY. 1775–1800

Until the sixteenth century, corpses were sewn into canvas bags and buried next to the church walls. Later, coffins came into use and separate graveyards were set off next to the church.

Originally white, not black, was the color of mourning. In this drawing, the man's cloak and the sash on his hat are black, but the coat, waistcoat, and tie are white. The woman's white hat and the white kerchief tied around it are the only parts of her costume that indicate that she, too, is in mourning.

GYPSIES

ALSACE. 1775–1800

In spite of the new police forces organized by the Enlightened Absolutism to deal with gypsies and other vagabonds, the gypsies still wandered through the European countries. In their own bands or as members of gangs of robbers, they were an affliction of the century. In countries like Germany and Italy, which were split into innumerable small political territories, they were particularly difficult to control.

TOWNSFOLK FROM BERLIN

GERMANY. LATE EIGHTEENTH CENTURY

In the old Prussian spirit of frugality, the costume of Berliners was marked by great simplicity, with little finesse in color or cut. The heavily padded black coat of the woman on the right was a style often worn by female peddlers. The hat was made of black straw with a black or red ribbon. Children were still dressed like little adults.

Daniel Chodowiecki, an engraver from Berlin's middle class, who lived from 1726 to 1801, was a keen observer of his fellow townspeople. His work was the costume source for this and several other drawings.

BUTCHER AND TOWNSWOMAN
GERMANY. END OF EIGHTEENTH CENTURY

In Germany, there were butchers and butchers, each with their separate guild. The man in this drawing, who offers a sausage for inspection by his client, belonged to the Schweinsmetzger, a group of pork butchers who made sausages and similar products. There was also the Altmetzger, or oldtime butcher, who dealt in all kinds of meats. The Brandmetzger went from village to village offering his services as a slaughterer to individual peasants, while the Wirts-metzger was permanently employed by one of the bigger inns.

The guilds were always careful to see that these boundaries were observed and also that competition within them was kept down to a certain level. Thus, a butcher in Gotha whose sausages might be in demand as far away as Berlin, was purposely limited to a certain amount of slaughtering.

STREET VENDORS

BERLIN. END OF EIGHTEENTH CENTURY

There is no dearth of information about the appearance of the characters who roamed the streets of Europe during this period. Following the example of the old *Cris de Paris*, it was the vogue to publish collections of drawings showing the lives of the city people; we can find these for London, Madrid, Vienna, Danzig, Naples, and other cities. They all testify to the fact that urban dress had become uniform all over Europe.

TUSCAN PEASANTS

ITALY. END OF EIGHTEENTH CENTURY

Peasants in Tuscany were better off than in any other part of Italy except Piedmont. Tuscan girls, noted a contemporary writer, were "very beautiful, more than the Romans, with good complexions and sparkling eyes, attractively dressed, their big hats decorated with colored ribbons and artificial flowers, and in general looking like the village girls in a French opera." They were also called "quite coquettish but very properly behaved."

The man's stiff hat is of a style much worn by the common man in Italy during this era. It stems from the hats worn by the drivers of stagecoaches in France and Germany.

PEASANTS

Despite their infinite variety, the many peasant costumes of the eighteenth century, and later, undeniably have much in common. All of their essential elements were retentions of urban costume, and although the peasants of different regions retained these elements independently, the fact is that all rural costume in the seventeenth and eighteenth centuries shows related traces.

Thus, for example, the trousers of the boy in this drawing are of a type fashionable in the towns more than a hundred years earlier, but still worn by peasant boys in such distant regions as Iceland (page 318), Germany (page 321), Bohemia (page 335), and many other places. Of the two costumes here, only the boy's is strongly Danish in flavor.

PEASANT WOMEN

NORWAY. END OF EIGHTEENTH CENTURY

Norwegians were the most independent peasants in all Europe. Like other Scandinavian countries, Norway had an infinite variety of regional costumes. In this drawing, the headgear, jackets, apron strings, and the shoes on the woman on the right are strongly Norwegian in character.

PEASANTS FROM LIMOGES
FRANCE. END OF EIGHTEENTH CENTURY

The zigzag decorations on the girl's bodice and skirt are regional to her part of France. The outfit of the man in this drawing is quite typical of that worn by any French common man of his day. He is wearing the short justaucorps with wide cuffs, a style by now old-fashioned, and a waistcoat and culottes. He has pulled his long stockings up over the knees of his culottes, a practice common to workingmen in the city as well as the country. His broad, flat hat was more typical of the peasant than the townsman.

The wide, flat collar known as the falling band went out of style with townsmen more than a hundred years ago. By now it has been dropped in favor of the knotted cravat by peasants too. The townsman's cravat would be white, often decorated with embroidery or a woven design. The peasant's cravat was usually red or black.

TOWNSWOMEN

PARIS. 1775–1800

The women in this drawing belong to a group of destitutes, estimated as between 30,000 and 60,000, who played a major role in the revolution. In the beginning, they formed a driving element in the crowd that forced the return of the royal family from Versailles. Later, they roamed the streets in wolfpacks, almost insane and often drunk, reviling and assaulting anyone who appeared to them to be an aristocrat. During the terror, they attended the trials en masse, calling for the death sentence. Surrounding the guillotine, they knitted while they watched the executions.

SANSCULOTTES

FRANCE. END OF EIGHTEENTH CENTURY

The red Phrygian cap, once the mark of the sailor, has now become a symbol of the revolutionary, particularly of the members of the Jacobin club, the strongest and most radical influence in the Sections of Paris, and a decisive force both in sporadic uprisings and during the Terror.

The long sailors' trousers—the man on the left is wearing only remnants of them—gave these men the name of sansculottes. In spite of popular misconception, the name did not apply to people who did not wear pants at all, but, rather, to people who did not wear culottes, the tight, knee-length breeches associated with upper classes, but sometimes worn by lower-class men, too. The trousers of the sansculottes were sometimes striped in the colors of the revolution, red, white, and blue, or they were of unbleached linen. Basically, they are the same trousers worn by men today.

A GUIDE
TO THE PICTURES